HUMMINGBIRDS DON'T FLY IN THE RAIN

A MOTHER'S EXTRAORDINARY SEARCH FOR HER DAUGHTER— IN THIS LIFE AND THE NEXT

KIMBERLY KLEIN

"A riveting story of unimaginable heartbreak and courage. It leaves you in awe of this mother's vast ability to love and to heal. It cannot help but change your view of what is possible."

—ELLEN SIMON, SCREENWRITER, *ONE FINE DAY*
AND *MOONLIGHT AND VALENTINO*

"The story is compelling, fascinating and riveting—I couldn't put it down! The chapter on 'Raising Talia' is one of the most intriguing accounts of parenting I've ever read."

—JENNIFER READ HAWTHORNE, #1 *NEW YORK TIMES* BESTSELLING
CO-AUTHOR OF *CHICKEN SOUP FOR THE WOMAN'S SOUL*
AND *CHICKEN SOUP FOR THE MOTHER'S SOUL*

"This spellbinding, true story shows how the human spirit can triumph in the face of adversity with some inspiring help from beyond the veil."

—RANDY PEYSER, AUTHOR OF *THE POWER OF MIRACLE THINKING*

For Talia
My sweet sugarplum; you will always be my
greatest love, joy and inspiration.

Portrait of Talia in oil by Fred Kepler

For information about this title or to order other books and/or electronic media, contact the publisher:
Pretty Much Amazing Press, a division of PMA Content Group
Pahrump, Nevada
www.prettymuchamazingpress.com
1-800-650-6422

Library of Congress Control Number: 2011912907

ISBN (paperback): 978-0-9837750-0-3
ISBN (hardcover): 978-0-9837750-1-0

Printed in the United States of America

Cover and Interior design by: 1106 Design

Author Photo: Peter Palladino   Make up: Marie Augustine

DISCLAIMER

This book is based on my life with my daughter, her father, and our families. Everything in this book is true as to how I lived it, perceived it, and experienced it.

Contents

PART ONE
THE CALL

CHAPTER ONE

DECEMBER 23

It was about 3:30 in the afternoon of December 23, 2007 when the phone rang. I had just finished watching *Black Beauty* and was thinking what a cute movie it was, and how I could hardly wait for Talia to be home the next night so we could start our holiday break. I picked up the phone; it was Bob Klein, my ex-husband Michael's father.

"Kim, something terrible has happened. The plane with Michael and Frankie—"

My mouth went dry. "What about Talia? Where's Talia?" I pleaded, not understanding why he hadn't mentioned my daughter—his granddaughter—only her friend, Francesca Lewis.

"Talia was with Michael and Frankie, but their plane never landed in Volcan. It's missing."

My heart stopped. My brain stopped. I stared into space with the phone at my ear, unable to speak. Like a robot I moved from the den to my office and sat down at the computer.

"What should I do? I have to go to Panama!"

Bob said, "Yes, you probably should go."

"What's going on in Panama now? Who's looking for the plane?"

He said Michael's brother-in-law, Jim, was organizing a search.

My mind felt empty, as if someone had unplugged it. Mechanically, I asked him what airlines went to Panama, even though I already knew the answer. He told me Copa and Continental flew direct from Los Angeles International Airport (LAX) to Panama City, then asked if I would call the Lewises. I could hardly figure out how to turn my computer on, much less dial the Lewises' number. He said he'd do it, and we hung up.

I was so frightened for Talia that I didn't even know what to pack. I grabbed my passport and stuck it in my backpack, then threw in some underwear and two shirts. I forgot my toothbrush, pajamas, any pants besides the jeans I had on, and my cell phone charger. *That* would end up being a big deal.

It would be a two-hour drive to LAX from Santa Barbara. I decided I'd start making calls, including to the airlines, once I was on the freeway—I had to get going. But first, I needed to make sure Frankie's parents knew. Bob had not reached them yet, so I tried their house—no answer. Then I called Frankie's mother on her cell phone. No answer. I left a message. "Valerie, this is Kim. Give me a call as soon as you can. Thanks." That was it. I could not leave the information on her voicemail.

I ran out of the house. Just then, Valerie called me back. I had no idea what to say or how to say it, but I had to tell her. "Valerie, I don't know how to say this except to be straight. The plane the kids were on from the islands to Volcan is missing. It didn't land when it was supposed to. I'm heading to Panama right now. Do you want to come with me?"

Valerie was in shock, as I expected she would be. Unsure what to do, she said she had to call Kirk, her husband. "I'm going to Panama tonight," I said. "I'm trying to get reservations, and I need to know who's going so I can get reservations for you too." I told her to keep me posted.

Once in the car, I called Linda, Michael's sister, who had first called Bob about the missing plane. She and her husband, Jim, lived in the city of David on the Pacific side of Panama, where Michael owned a string of islands called Islas Secas. He had taken Talia and Frankie to his eco-resort there.

I wanted to find out from Linda exactly what had happened. When had she found out the plane was missing, who had told her, what was being done right now to look for the plane—whether there was any news at all.

Linda had no information for me. All she knew was that Michael had been flying to his friend Calle Jansen's coffee plantation that day. Calle had left a message on her answering machine that the plane had not shown up at the landing strip. Linda hadn't gotten home until 5:30 p.m., so she had no idea what time Calle had left the message. She didn't know whether he had called the authorities or started a search, but she was thinking Michael had "pulled a Michael" and decided to change his plans without letting anyone know. She figured eventually he would call from somewhere else and say he had decided to do this or that.

I knew this was not the case. First, Talia would have called to tell me about the change—she always calls me, always. Second, Talia and Michael had definite plans, and their date of return, December 24, was set in stone. Michael would not alter that.

I asked Linda how I should to get to David once I landed in Panama City. She said her dad was flying in, and they had arranged for a driver to meet him at the international airport. They weren't sure whether he would then go to the regional airport and take a commuter flight to David or travel by car.

I had no idea Bob was going to Panama! He had never mentioned it in our conversations—not when I had told him I had to get there or when I had asked about the different airlines. Not even when I had called him for Linda's phone number. I was flabbergasted that Bob hadn't offered to make reservations for me on his flight. If the tables had been turned, there's no question I would have made reservations for him.

It was now about 4:30 p.m., and I was still on the freeway, frantically trying to get some sort of reservations to Panama that night. I couldn't get through to Copa, so I called American Express Travel for help. They were able to get me a reservation on a Delta flight that went through New York and arrived at Tocumen International Airport in Panama City around 2:00 p.m. the next day. I took it.

Right after I hung up, Bob called. He said he was getting ready to head to LAX and thought he would see if we could drive together. "No use both of us driving," is what he said. He had been totally selfish; now he wanted to carpool. As if gas consumption was what mattered! It wasn't that he needed company in this time of need—and it wasn't that he cared about me while I was freaking out about the safety of my daughter, her father and her friend.

Bob told me he was taking a Copa fight that left LAX at 1:15 a.m. and got into Panama City around 10:30 the next morning. From there he would go to the Marcos A. Gelabert regional airport, also known as Albrook, and try to get on a late-afternoon flight to David. If he couldn't get on one of those flights, it would be an eight-hour drive to David. At this point he wasn't sure how he was getting there.

Well, I did know how I was getting to David. After talking to Linda, it was pretty clear I needed to find my own transportation. I wasn't going to risk being stuck in Panama City. I didn't speak more than ten words of Spanish, and at this point I was so upset I could barely speak English.

I called a friend of mine, Rob, who had some Panamanian connections, and asked him for the name of a pilot who could fly me from Panama City to David. Rob gave me the phone number of Rodolfo, a pilot he knew. When I told Rodolfo my name, he already knew why I was calling. Michael was famous in Panama; he was known as Mr. Michael, the wealthy and powerful figure who had built the eco-resort on the Islas Secas. Everyone had either worked for him or knew a friend or relative who had worked for him.

Rodolfo told me he had been planning to search the area where the plane had gone missing the next morning. He said he would come back to Panama City around noon and fly me to David whenever my plane got in. Thank goodness!

Still on the way to LAX, I decided to try to get on the same Copa flight Bob was on. American Express tried to reach Copa while I was on the line. At first Copa wasn't answering—it was the middle of the night in Panama. When someone did finally answer, my phone kept going in and out of reception. It was hell.

Finally, the American Express representative said they were able to get me on the waiting list for the Copa flight Bob was on. Even after telling them why I was heading down, that was the best they could do. At least I had a backup ticket on Delta, but that flight would get me to Panama City at least four hours after Bob arrived. Knowing what I now know about Bob, that four-hour delay could have prevented me from ever getting to the search headquarters in Boquete. I would have landed in Panama City without anyone to meet me, and when I arrived in David, I wouldn't have known where to go. I would have been completely forgotten.

Once I had arrangements on Copa, I phoned my brother, Justin, whom I always call J. I didn't want to call my mom yet. I couldn't. I knew I wouldn't be able to get the words out; I would break down, and she would get hysterical.

J. was visiting with his boys in South Carolina when I called. He said he couldn't talk and hung up. I called right back. He said, "I can't talk, I'm in church." I said, "It's an emergency! Talia's plane is missing in Panama." He was stunned. He asked if he should meet me in Panama. I was too distraught to know what to do; I couldn't tell him a thing. I was barely able to make it there myself. J. said his passport was in L.A., so he would fly home immediately to pick it up, then fly to Panama. I told him to wait; I would call if I needed him.

I then called my dad, who lived in Ventura. I had to tell him. I knew he would want to come with me to Panama, but because of his heart problems, I felt he shouldn't. He asked me to stop off at his boat on the way to LAX, though, so he could give me some cash to take. All I had were credit cards and my ATM card, so I picked up a bundle of money from my father and headed down. We figured I would need to pay people to get me where I needed to go, and cash always works.

I also called my friend Merryl. She wanted to go with me, but I told her no. Although she spoke fluent Spanish, I knew the situation would be too intense, too frantic, and I didn't need to worry about anyone except Talia and myself.

At this point I was thinking the plane must have had to make an emergency landing, and Talia and Michael and Frankie were stuck in some field or on a hillside with no cell coverage, waiting for us to find them. That is what I really thought. I knew Talia was extremely smart and would act wisely, not because she had ever been in an emergency, but because I had always told her what to do in case of one. We had watched survival shows, and she had gone to child safety classes. I just knew she was sitting there saying to everyone, "My mom *will* be here. She will come for us, no doubt, so we just need to stay put so we don't get lost or hurt. Hang out and she *will* be here as soon as she can." That's how she and I were. She knew she could rely on me for *everything*.

I also knew she probably feared for her life. I recalled the time she was driving home from Tucson with her dad and his girlfriend and her kids. They had just left some little diner in a roadside town on I-10, when Talia noticed her dad looking in the mirror a lot and speeding up. He was going over 120 miles per hour when she noticed they were being followed.

She asked her dad about this, but he ignored her. It was at this moment that I started to get one text message after another from Talia. *I love you, Mommy. Love you so much . . .* I knew something was up but wasn't sure what.

That night, when Talia was in bed and I lay next to her, talking, she burst into tears and told me what had happened. She said she had thought they were going to be killed and she would never see me again.

It was during this conversation that I told Talia that no matter what happened, no matter where on earth she was, no matter what, I would come for her. I would find her, and I would bring her home. Nothing would stop me, nothing.

Knowing Talia would text me from wherever they had crash landed—if she had cell reception—I realized she had to be out of cell range. She would be scared, more scared than anyone could possibly imagine, but she would be confident I would be there for her the second I could. This would keep her strong and allow her to get through anything. She wouldn't let herself give up. It was important that I knew this, in case she had some kind of injury. I knew she had the physical *and* mental strength to make it through.

When I was almost at the airport, I finally felt I could take a breath and call my mom. I waited until the last minute, because I was sure she was going to freak out. However, she was actually calm. I think she knew I needed to be calm, and this was how she could help me.

I also called Talia's riding trainer, Leslie, who had become my good friend. She got very upset. Her husband, Dan, told me he was coming with me to Panama—and for some reason, I said OK. He was young and easygoing, spoke Spanish, and could take care of himself. I wouldn't need to worry about him while I was worrying about Talia. There was time for him to get to LAX because my flight on Delta was not leaving until 11:00 p.m., but he had to leave right away.

After all these calls, I realized I had not packed my cell phone charger! I had my car charger but no wall charger. This was going to be a problem unless I could buy one at the airport. Just as I realized this, my mom called and told me my cousin Sharon, who lives in the San Fernando Valley, was coming to LAX to wait with me so I wouldn't be alone. She would try to find me a charger on the way.

I spoke to Valerie again, and she told me her family was heading down to LAX to try to get on a flight to Panama. By the time they had called Delta, about two hours after I offered to do it, the flight was already sold out. Copa was also completely booked, so they were going to try to work something out at the airport. Valerie and Kirk, their daughter Rosie, and Kirk's brother Peter were all going. That was a lot of people to get booked on a flight last minute.

At LAX I dropped my car off in a parking lot, took a shuttle to the Delta counter, and bought the Delta ticket that American Express had held for me. I had also reserved a ticket for Dan, who was on his way down from Santa Barbara. I planned to pay for his ticket as soon as I knew for sure that I was taking the Delta flight. My goal was to get onto Bob's Copa flight, but I needed to get processed for the 11:00 p.m. Delta flight in case I didn't make it on the Copa flight. I couldn't take the chance of having *no* flight!

After I finished at Delta, I ran down to the Copa counter in the next building over. It was now 7:00 or 8:00 p.m., and a huge line was already forming, even though the counter wouldn't open until 9:00 p.m. I spent that time in line trying to hold back my tears. I called my mom, my dad, my brother, and friends like Georgette, Ray, and Merryl again. Everyone wanted to come with me. But I didn't want any of them at this point. I figured I could handle it myself. I thought I would be there with Bob and Linda and it would be OK. I was so, so wrong about this one.

While standing in line I decided that if the Copa agents couldn't get me on the flight, I would try to find someone in line who would agree to sell me his or her ticket. I figured a bribe would work. I *had* to get there as soon as possible.

The Copa counter opened, and the line slowly began to move. Just then, my cousin Sharon and her husband, Mark, showed up. The minute I saw them I broke down. They hadn't been able to get me a charger because they couldn't find a cell phone store that was open, but I was so glad they were there. I was so scared for Talia. This was something *no one* should ever have to go through.

A few minutes later, I noticed Bob had arrived. He was standing at the back of the line, and I did what any family member would do—I brought him up to my place. Oddly, when I went to get him, he said hello but didn't hug me or reach out to me. His son and my daughter—his granddaughter—were missing, and he didn't even hug me! Nevertheless, I told him to come up with me, and he did.

When it was my turn at the Copa counter, I had Bob check in with me because I thought it might help me get a ticket. He had already bought his ticket on Copa, and I was on the waiting list. I immediately told the Copa representative, who was a very nice woman, that I had to get on this flight. I explained that Talia's plane was missing and I had to get there ASAP to search. I told her my father-in-law was on this flight, and I had to be on it with him. She disappeared for about ten minutes and came back and issued me a ticket! I was incredibly grateful to her.

Now I could breathe for a second: I was on the Copa flight. There was no way I could get Dan on the flight, so I called him and said I really appreciated his efforts and his love, but he would have to turn around and go home. He didn't want to but did it anyway. I also let Valerie know that I couldn't get them any seats on the flight. Valerie said they were almost at the airport and would take care of it when they arrived.

I thanked my cousins and hugged them, crying. Then Bob and I headed up through security. After that, we went to a little sandwich shop. Bob picked up his food and paid for it. That was when I knew I was in for a very cold and distant time with him in Panama: he didn't even offer to pay for my sandwich! Bob is a retired physician, a very successful specialist with millions of dollars invested in Michael's hedge fund. Money was not Bob's problem. His problem was coldheartedness.

After buying some food, I headed over to the little airport store to look for a phone charger. They had nothing. I could not be in the jungle or in the middle of nowhere, waiting for Talia to call and tell me she was OK, and not have a phone! I was able to find various charging parts, and after buying three different packs of things, I managed to piece together a very short charger with a cord no more than eighteen inches long. Thank God I had something! I then grabbed about fifteen protein bars and a few bottles of water. I was going to need these to give to Talia, Frankie, and Michael when we found them. They would be hungry, weak, and dehydrated.

I then ran all over the gate area looking for an electrical outlet. When I found one, I sat down, plugged in, and tried to relax a bit. Bob walked by. He didn't see me, but I called him over. He said he was going to sit by the gate. He had some sleeping pills, and he gave me one. I took out my water and stuck the pill in my mouth. As I swallowed it, Bob said, "Oh, you need to wait until thirty minutes before the flight." The flight was in ninety minutes.

Now I was going to fall asleep in the airport. Thanks for the warning, Bob! I kept myself awake out of fear of what Talia was going through. I was afraid she might be in a dangerous place; I was afraid she was not sitting there waiting for me to find her but was lying there, hurt, in pain or worse. Whenever that thought entered my mind, I tried to get rid of it quickly, as it made me cry. Thinking Talia was OK, just waiting for me, was a much better thought. But honestly, I wasn't able to control my thoughts very well.

As it got closer to boarding time, Kirk called and told me they were at the airport. They had booked a flight, but somehow the reservations hadn't been held for them—and now the flight was full. They were freaking out, and I didn't blame them. I told them I would see what I could do. As soon as the Copa agents arrived at our gate, I went up to one of them and told him the situation.

I told him my daughter and her dad and her friend were on a missing plane, and I had to get the friend's parents on this flight so they could search for their daughter. Bob, by the way, was asleep in his chair. I then took out my cell phone and showed the man a photo of Talia and Michael.

Immediately he said, "I know them! He's on my flight all the time, and I remember them on my flight a couple of days ago." That was amazing! He said he would get Frankie's parents on our flight. He called down to the ticket counter and spoke with someone, and within minutes all the Lewises had tickets and were being ushered up through security, past the huge lines, to our gate. Thank God I was able to get them on that plane!

The plane was fully boarded by the time the Lewises made it up to the gate. I was in my seat, and Bob was a few rows back, so I wasn't able to talk to Valerie before the flight. I did see that they all made it onto the plane, which was my main concern. Now there was nothing I could do for the next six or eight hours but wait and hope.

I lay back and tried to sleep. I was absolutely sure that when I got off the plane in Panama City, I would have a voicemail from Talia, telling me they had crashed but were totally fine, and she had just now gotten to a place where she had cell reception. That was the thought that kept me sane for the moment. That was the thought I would keep in my head while I was on the plane.

CHAPTER TWO

DECEMBER 24

Somehow the sleeping pill worked. I think my mind and body knew that whatever sleep I got on that plane might be the last for quite a while, so I had to sleep. And I did. But it's interesting how your body knows when to wake up. Just before the flight attendant came around to ensure that all of our seat backs were in an upright position, I woke up, ready to start my search. I figured once we landed in Panama City, it would be all action. Fast going from one airport to the other, fast getting on the charter flight to David, and fast getting to the search and rescue control center.

Even before the flight attendant said we could use cell phones, I turned mine on. We hadn't hit the ground yet, but I figured we were close enough to get a signal. I just knew that I would see the little voicemail icon showing I had a message from Talia, telling me she was OK. But I didn't. I had *no messages!* I was stunned.

I waited for permission to use my cell phone, then quickly called Rodolfo to let him know I was in Panama City and would be heading to the regional airport as soon as possible. I asked him how many passengers his plane could hold, now that I had Bob and the Lewises with me. He said all but one would fit on his plane.

The Lewises decided Peter would be the one to take a commercial flight to David, as he was capable of figuring things out on his own. It would later prove to be a good choice; on that flight Peter met a prominent businessman from David who gave up his holiday with his family to help us.

Linda had arranged for a driver to take Bob to the regional airport. He said I could ride with him, and I invited him to share the charter flight I had arranged from Panama City to David. We cleared customs and waited outside the secured area for the driver and the Lewises. It was clear Bob didn't want to wait for the Lewises, but I insisted we wait and go to the other airport together.

The Lewises finally cleared customs, and we all walked to the parking lot, where the driver was waiting for us—in a pickup truck! Four of us crammed into the cab, sitting on each other's laps, while Kirk and Peter sat in the open back with the suitcases.

It took us about forty-five minutes to drive through the city. More precious time went by as the driver made numerous calls trying to figure out where to take us; he even called Rodolfo, our pilot—it turns out everyone in Panama knows one another! But in the end, there was no hurry. We had to wait another hour and a half for Rodolfo, who had told me he was on his way when we had talked earlier. It seemed nobody felt the urgency I did.

My phone was not holding its charge well at all, so while we waited, I scouted around and found an electrical outlet for my phone, right next to a room that looked like an air-conditioned phone booth with an ATM machine in it. I leaned up against the windows of that little room, pressing my face against the glass and trying to stay cool while I charged my phone.

Gradually, everyone in our group began moving through some glass doors into the main waiting area. Not wanting to be left alone, I followed them and found another outlet across the room from everyone. I was only twenty feet away, but I have never felt so alone in my life. I let my phone charge for as long as I could stand it, and then went over to where Bob was.

No one spoke much. Bob started getting agitated because Rodolfo wasn't there and kept insisting we take a commercial flight instead. I wanted to tell him to get on a commercial flight himself, but instead reassured him that Rodolfo was on his way. I was trying to be calm, concentrating on getting to Talia, but the truth was that I was completely freaked out because I still hadn't received a voicemail from her telling me she was OK.

Finally Rodolfo landed at the airport. An airport worker, or one of Rodolfo's helpers, found us in the waiting area and led us out to the plane while Rodolfo fueled up. Peter stayed behind to take the next commercial flight out.

The flight to David was difficult. I looked out at the land below, not knowing where I was or where they had flown, and tried to spot Talia's plane on the ground somewhere. I really thought I would look down and see something—a plane on a field where it should not be—and it would be them!

But soon after we took off, the sky became cloudy and I couldn't see a thing. Until the last ten minutes of the flight, when we made our descent, it was nothing but solid clouds. I thought they were just normal clouds; I didn't realize there had been a storm. I couldn't see an inch in front of my face as I pressed against the plane's window. I was feeling helpless and sick. It wasn't the plane ride that was making me nauseous; it was the thought of Talia being out there, possibly hurt, tired, hungry, scared, alone.

I wondered if Michael was hurt or worse, and I realized that Talia might be trying to keep herself and Frankie safe while they waited for me to come for them. I tried to stay calm. Sitting on the plane was very, very hard.

As we descended into David, I looked down at the airport and saw *no activity*. This airport was close to the area where we needed to search—the mountains near the Baru volcano, where Calle lived on his coffee plantation in Volcan. I expected planes and helicopters to be fueling up, taking off and landing, as they do in the U.S. when a plane is lost. But there was nothing going on! I couldn't believe it. There had to be a reason the airport was deserted.

The airport itself looked the way I had imagined it. Talia had flown into this airport many times with her dad, and she had told me about the place. She said that when her dad's jet landed, people would stop their cars outside the fence and watch as the jet taxied to a stop. She told me the people of David had never seen a private jet until her dad started flying into that airport on his way to the islands. She said everyone there thought of Michael as a king. They did everything and anything for him.

When we got off the plane, a man met us, and we followed him to an outdoor corridor leading to what seemed like the airport offices. *No one* was there—not one airport official, security guard, spectator, or search and rescue person. Then, out of a door that led to what looked like the control tower, Linda came out to greet us. She was holding her baby, Talia's cousin Catalina, just over a year old.

We were all very quiet. Bob and I hugged Linda and introduced her to Frankie's family. Then Jim, Linda's husband, whom I had never met, came out of the building to see us. I went up to him, hugged him, and introduced myself. He seemed a bit cold, but I associated his distance with trying to stay businesslike and focused on the search—except there was no search.

"What's going on? Where are all the planes?" I asked, totally confused about why nothing seemed to be happening. Jim explained that the weather was too bad to do air searches, and the ground search was being orchestrated at a Panamanian volunteer search office in Boquete, about an hour from David.

Immediately, right there in the outdoor hall of the airport, I told Jim we needed to offer a reward. Both he and Linda were horrified. "This is Panama! You can't offer a reward—all the freaks will come out!"

How is this possible? I thought. *My daughter—Bob's granddaughter, Linda's niece—is missing; Michael—Bob's son, Linda's brother—is missing; Frankie Lewis is missing; and they won't let me offer a reward? First of all, I want as many people out there looking for that plane as possible, crazy people or not. If someone saw something, I want to know. If someone is holding them all for ransom, I want them to contact us so I can get my daughter and the others back.*

But I didn't want to start an argument. I had just landed and hadn't been with them more than two minutes. I decided to wait and assess the situation for myself.

The man who had met us then directed us to a big room upstairs, overlooking the runway. They wanted to bring us lunch! *What is happening?* I thought. *This isn't a vacation; every second counts in the search!* I wasn't about to sit in some room at the airport where nothing was going on and have lunch. I wanted to get in a car or a plane—anything that would take me closer to Talia. But I was powerless on my own. I surrendered and went upstairs with the others.

A few minutes after we sat down upstairs, Rodolfo came in and told us that the charge for the charter flight was $1,500. I had never asked him how much it was going to be because it hadn't mattered—all that mattered was that I got to where I needed to be in order to start looking for Talia. It seemed a bit high for a short flight, but it was what it was. Bob looked at the Lewises and me and suggested we split the bill three ways.

Rodolfo didn't accept American Express, and I didn't want to use up so much cash right at the start of my search, so I asked Bob to pay my third and told him I would pay him back. He did, and the Lewises paid the other third.

Soon Jim came up to the room and started talking quietly to Linda. I overheard him say he was heading to Boquete—I immediately said I was going with him. I needed to see what was being done to find my daughter; I needed to be in on the search! He said he was leaving immediately, so I grabbed my backpack and followed him. As I was heading downstairs after him, I heard Linda call to Jim that her dad was coming too. The Lewises decided to wait at the airport for Peter—but I was getting out of there. I had to get to Talia!

Bob and I got into Jim's truck. The ride to Boquete took close to an hour. During that time Jim told us again that they hadn't been able to use search planes because the weather was so bad. That was why no one had searched the day before—the day the plane went missing. *How can that be?* I thought. *In America we have planes that fly in the wind, rain, and clouds with special infrared equipment.*

He also said that because of the Christmas holiday, nobody was available for a ground search. He and Linda hadn't known the plane was missing until evening the previous day, long after it had disappeared. And at the time, they thought it was a very real possibility that Michael had decided to go somewhere else and not tell anyone.

20

Then he dropped a bombshell: he said this storm had been predicted. In turmoil, I thought to myself, *If the weather was too bad to search, why did Michael's plane go up in the first place? If the clouds were so thick, why did they fly into them?*

I tried to keep my mind from going anywhere except to think that they had had some engine problems and landed in a field, out of cell range. I tried really hard not to think of any other possibilities. I just stared out the windows as we climbed higher in elevation, heading for the little mountain town of Boquete.

I was not prepared for what I saw next. The roads in Boquete were mostly dirt and full of potholes. What little asphalt there was on the roadway was so old it was basically nonexistent. I had expected to see a true search and rescue headquarters, stocked with searchers, equipment—and a lot of action. Instead, the place looked like a junkyard, with old cars parked along the fence, mud puddles, cracked walkways, and a narrow cement and dirt path that led up to a little white building. There was no one around.

We parked and went into the building. The office was one small room with a desk, a blackboard, a big map of the area on the wall, an old Mr. Coffee machine, some file cabinets, an old TV, and a phone. There were only a couple of men standing around. I thought, *Where is everyone? Who is looking for my daughter?* I thought I would go out of my mind. I was ready to hop into a Jeep and head into the mountains myself.

Jim introduced us to the head of the volunteer search group. He stood looking at us silently, until I couldn't take it any more and asked, "What's going on? Who's out looking for my daughter's plane?"

The man confirmed what Jim had told us earlier: not a single person was out looking for Talia and the others! Because it was

Christmas Eve and the weather was bad, everyone was at home. In other words, there was no official Panamanian rescue team.

Jim told him we *had* to have men and offered to pay about twelve dollars to each man willing to search—twelve dollars a *day*, plus expenses, like gas, rental fees for trucks and ATVs, and so on. *Why so little?* I thought. When I questioned him about the fee, he told me the Panamanians don't make much each day, so this was a lot of money for them.

I again mentioned a reward. *No one* was searching, and I wanted people out there. Clearly they needed an incentive to leave their houses and come out to search. But again Jim yelled, "No, you can't do that here!" Bob agreed.

It was then I realized that I was alone with these people; I had no family of my own with me. I was stuck with Bob and Jim, and they had already started to show their lack of consideration for anything I had to say. It was the worst feeling I've ever had, being alone in a strange place with cold, heartless people who had absolutely no regard for me, while my daughter, my only child, the love of my life, was missing, I couldn't comprehend what was happening; I wanted to throw up, I wanted to scream, I wanted to cry.

To make matters worse, I heard Jim tell Bob he had spoken earlier to Kieren, the manager of Michael's Islas Secas resort, who had told him that the takeoff of Talia and Michael's plane was the worst he had ever seen. The plane had dropped off the runway and almost crashed into the ocean before gaining enough altitude to continue flying. It was so bad that Kieren had called the charter company and told them never to send that pilot again.

This sent my anxiety into overdrive. The plane had nearly crashed on takeoff, and they had not turned around and landed immediately? What was wrong with them? Then they continued to fly over the ocean and bypassed another airstrip, at David, while heading directly into a storm? There was something seriously wrong here.

At this point Linda and the Lewises showed up in Boquete with Peter. The businessman Peter had met on the plane had driven them to search headquarters, then stayed to help them with translations and phone calls for help.

One of the men showed us the map on the wall. We had been so distracted, talking with the head searchers and discussing a reward, that we hadn't noticed it. We all stood inside that little rescue office, staring at the map, which had a few red marks indicating where people thought they had seen something. I found I was looking at a huge mountain range, not a flat area of farms and fields as I had expected.

Then another American came in. This was Sam Taliaferro, who had moved to Panama and opened a resort in Boquete. Sam was an amazing person who would prove to be instrumental in the search and a wonderful help to us.

Sam was wet and dirty. He had just come off the mountain with his son, Justin. They had heard about the missing plane and had taken it upon themselves to search and gather information. Sam had taken his ATV up one side of the volcanic mountain range while his son went up another way, searching for the plane and for witnesses. On the way up they had questioned a group of Panamanian Indians who lived on the mountain, gathering information about different sightings of the plane. After being out in the elements for several hours, Sam had now come down to search headquarters.

It seemed there had been a lot of sightings of the plane. People saw it here, then there, in the clouds, out of the clouds, low, high. One man said he thought the wings of the plane were shimmying from the wind. Sam added all the information about the sightings to the big map on the wall.

It began to look like a real search and rescue map, with triangulations everywhere. We now had a pretty good idea where to look for the plane; the southwest part of the mountain range was where we should be sending people.

But what people? I started to panic. We now thought we knew where to look, but no one was looking. And it was evening! Talia was out there in the wilderness, cold, hungry, scared for her life. Again, I felt sick.

I heard Linda talking to Calle on the phone; he had organized a search party of his own. He had gathered his plantation workers and some others and had supplied them with ATVs, trucks, and other equipment. He would pay them a salary to search from his side of the mountain, close to his plantation. His search team would go up the northwest side of the mountain from the Volcan area and come down toward the southwest portion. Whatever search group we were able to assemble would start at the bottom of the southwest portion and go north. We would meet up with Calle's group at some point in the middle. At least that was the plan.

The problem was, none of this was going to start until the morning. It was now well over twenty-four hours since the plane had gone missing, and no one was out there! But Jim learned that the volunteers would show up to search in the morning, and, given the fact that it was nearly evening and nothing more could be done, I decided to wait until morning before doing anything different from what they had already planned.

I walked out to the porch of this little building just in time to hear Bob saying that if we did not find them soon, it would be too late. *Too late? Too late for what? What are you talking about!* I told Bob that people who've been in plane crashes have lived for weeks. A man and his kids were just lost in the snow for a week, and they were OK. He said something like, "I'm a doctor, and I know what I'm talking about. If they have injuries, their bodies will shut down after twenty-four hours, and then it will be too late."

I couldn't stand this. When I first found out the plane was missing, the only thing that helped at all was knowing the weather was moderate in Panama at this time of year, so Talia would not freeze, as she would have had they crashed in Alaska. And it was raining intermittently, so she would not go without water. No food was OK, but she had to have water. Now, not only did I have Bob telling me we had to get to them right away or they would die, but the weather was terrible—it was actually *cold* and windy and raining. And if they were up on the mountain, it was even colder!

My hopeful theory went out the window, and now I was faced with thoughts of Talia cold, hungry, scared for her life, sitting there all alone. Or maybe sitting there with her friend, her father or the pilot—even next to a dead body. Maybe she was hurt and dying, as Bob had described it.

But I couldn't tolerate these thoughts. I refused to let my mind go to any image other than Talia sitting there, waiting for me.

I began to assess the situation. It was the evening of December 24 and nothing was happening. We *hoped* that many men would come out of the woodwork in the early dawn hours to start a land search, and we were told that if the weather cleared, air searches could also start in the morning. This was all I had to hold onto.

But of course, this was just what we had been *told*. That was not enough for me. We needed to get real searchers, real search planes, helicopters, all the air support we could—*now*. The weather is never a factor in the U.S.; it wasn't going to stop me from finding my daughter in Panama.

My brother and I have a friend whose job is to organize groups of military and ex-military guys, a lot of them ex-Navy Seals, and contract them out for private security jobs. My brother suggested we call him to see if he could help us in some way. Great idea.

I called him. He answered immediately. He said he knew that Talia's plane was missing because of the news and because he'd heard from friends of ours. He'd been hoping I'd call.

"I need help!"

"What do you need? I'll help you in any way possible."

I told him the situation with the weather and the lack of men. I said we needed Black Hawks and men who could rappel out of them into the jungle.

Done. He had the group. He just needed to get hold of them. It was Christmas, after all, and these guys take holidays too. He asked if I could pay.

"*Yes*, I can pay. How much?" I didn't care how much it was; we were talking about my daughter's life, and her father's and Frankie's lives. I personally didn't have a lot of money; I would have to get some of it from Michael, his family, or his company— but I would do it.

"One million dollars," he said.

"What! OK, I'll find the money."

I knew Michael would pay anything to live; he would pay anything to save his daughter and her friend. I would get the money.

I called Steve, Michael's accountant at Pacificor, the hedge fund Michael owned and managed.

"Steve, I need one million dollars to pay the ex-Seals! There's no other way to save them."

Steve said he would get them the money, but he would need the authority of the executor of Michael's estate. He didn't know who that was, but I did—it was Bob. So I told Steve to call Gary, Michael's attorney. He would know who had the paperwork with this information. Meanwhile, I would talk to Bob. I knew it was going to be hard.

"Bob, I have a connection to a group of ex-Seals who can come in here with helicopters that can search in bad weather and at nighttime, with guys who can rappel down to lead searches. We need to hire them."

"How much?"

"One million dollars."

He hesitated. He told me that was a lot of money. *No shit, but it's my daughter and your son's life we're saving, and Michael would pay. We need to do this!* He said he had to think about it. He also said he didn't think he was the one to OK it, so I told him I knew he was the executor, and he was the one to make this call. All he had to do was let Steve know so he could move the money.

Bob didn't answer. Again, he said he would think about it. *Great. I have the guys and no money!* I couldn't say yes to them and hope to get the money; I didn't want to promise to pay and then not be able to. I told my connection I had to get back to him, that I was waiting for the authority to say yes to the money. What was wrong with Bob?

I went into the building for a moment, and when I came out, everyone was gone. Bob, Linda, and Jim had left. It turned out they had all gone back to Linda's house in David. They hadn't told me they were leaving or arranged for us to meet up in the morning. I was left with strangers, alone, to wonder about my daughter.

Sam was so kind. He made arrangements for the Lewises and me to stay at his resort and be closer to search headquarters.

On the way to his resort, Sam told us he had arranged for a helicopter to land at the resort at six o'clock the next morning, and we could go with them on the search. Finally, something was happening! I had something to look forward to in the morning. I would wake up, the storm would be over, the sun shining. I would get on that helicopter, and we would fly away. I would look out the windows and see the plane sitting there in a field or on top of the mountain in a clearing, and Talia would be standing outside the plane waving her hands, signaling the helicopter that she was OK. That is what I really hoped would happen.

Sam dropped us off at the restaurant area of the resort and said they would take care of us. But it was Christmas Eve. Families were having their holiday dinners, dressed up, joyous. We walked into the place in our worn jeans with messy hair and stressed looks on our faces. It was extremely difficult not to break down and cry, but I had to stay strong. I had to be the strong one to make sure Talia and the others were rescued.

The Lewises and I sat in the main part of the restaurant for quite awhile, waiting for a table. One never opened up. Finally, the restaurant people took us over to a private room just outside the main area and seated us. They told us all they had was turkey. OK, whatever they had was fine.

My phone, which was floating between barely having any battery life and the red zone, was ringing off the hook: media, family, friends, people I had never heard of. I was the only person in our group, consisting of Bob, the Lewises, and me, who had a cell phone that worked in Panama. I plugged the phone into an outlet on the floor and answered one of the calls. I had to crouch down, my face almost on the floor.

It was Kara, the parent of a girl in Talia and Frankie's class. "Kim, this is Kara, I heard Frankie is missing." *Hello! What about Talia?* I was so angry I hung up.

Then my phone rang again. It was Bob. He said he wanted to talk to the guy who was arranging the Seals to see if he was legitimate. I assured Bob that he was, but I said, "Of course you can call him." I gave Bob the phone number of my friend and hung up. A few minutes later I had a voicemail from Kara.

"Kim, this is Kara, I have a psychic, and she said she saw the plane heading toward the mountain and then turn left." This was consistent with what we thought we knew, but this was a psychic! Kara then said she saw a man and a girl holding hands, and they were fine. *OK, great. Talia and her dad are fine!* This message didn't really help me, but I was grasping at any hope I could find.

The phone rang again. It was Bob. He said he had spoken with my friend, and he seemed legitimate and nice. He would OK the money transfer, but it had to go directly to the guy, not to me. *Of course, Bob, what is your problem?* It was clear he didn't trust me, and that if he was going to give a million dollars away, he didn't want me having any contact with it. I didn't care; I wanted the guys paid, and I wanted them here ASAP, looking for my daughter! I knew if they got here they would find her.

Unfortunately, by the time Bob decided to OK this transaction, the group's "A" guys were gone, no longer an option. My friend had to scramble for a "B" set of men. He found a group he had never used before; they were guys someone else had recommended. I didn't care as long as I got some men and some helicopters here right away.

My friend said, "OK, the guys have a source who's located what they think is the plane. In the jungle. But they will not move without prepayment." The problem was, it was Christmas Eve, the bank was closed, and we had no ability to wire funds. It simply wasn't possible to get them the money in advance. It wasn't that we wouldn't do it, we simply couldn't.

The ex-Seals wouldn't budge. Bob then told them if they would give us the GPS coordinates for the plane, we'd give them $500,000 and they wouldn't have to come to Panama. I didn't agree with this. We needed them here! What good were coordinates if we couldn't get to them? We couldn't see through the clouds, and our rental helicopters couldn't fly in bad weather, in the dark, in the storm. We had nothing without the Black Hawks and the men!

During this "negotiation" with Bob, the guys decided not to take the job. It was all or nothing for them, so they backed out. We lost our hope! Bob claimed the guys were blackmailing him, but I don't really believe that. I think they got sick of his negotiations.

It was now nearly 11:00 p.m. We were in this strange restaurant, and I was face down on the floor, having phone conversations with Bob and anyone else that called, going back and forth to my table to take a few bites of food so I wouldn't pass out. I really had no appetite. Talia was hungry; how could I eat while my little daughter was starving out there!

We finished up and decided to go to our rooms and try to get some sleep. We had a very long day ahead, and we needed our strength to help with the search and to bring everyone back. When we went to the registration desk to get our keys, I noticed a couple of polo-type shirts for sale and bought both of them. I needed to have something to put on Talia and her dad or Frankie when we found them. They would be cold and probably wet.

I got to my room. I could not get myself to shower. *I cannot—I have to work on getting some help here!* I sat on the bed, calling people, anyone I thought could get us some help in Panama. I needed to find that plane! My brother's girlfriend had a friend who worked in Florida at the United States Southern Command, a military installation that controls all communications and satellite images in the area of the world we were in. She gave me his direct number, and I called him.

I don't remember his name, but he told me they have special radar that tracks the movement of all planes in Panama, and the satellite and radar information is kept for about a week. If he were to receive a directive from a superior, he would be able to get me that information. I had to get him that directive! The only person I knew who could accomplish this was the U.S. Embassy representative in Panama we had been talking to, Susan Armstrong.

I had had several very stressful, sometimes unpleasant conversations with Susan that day. Earlier, I had told her that Panama was totally incapable of putting on a search for Talia's plane, and that we needed help from the U.S. She kept telling me the U.S. had offered help to Panama in the search, but Panama had repeatedly rejected the help. *What was that about?* The head of the Panamanian search group insisted that his superior in Panama City had asked for help, but the U.S. wouldn't supply it. Someone was not telling the truth.

At first I thought the Panamanian government didn't want to admit that it was unable to conduct a real search and hadn't asked the U.S. at all, or, if it had asked, it had played down what it needed help with. Then I thought the U.S. wouldn't spend the money without a request for help from the Panamanian government.

I think the real story is that Panama wouldn't ask. The U.S. had resources in another Latin American country that could have been there in a few hours, once asked for. But the U.S. couldn't send in its military without permission. Personally, I didn't care where the help came from, I just needed it!

When I spoke to Susan Armstrong the next morning, she said she would look into my request to issue a directive to obtain radar information from the Southern Command. I don't think she ever did.

By now it was around 2:00 a.m., and I had to get some sleep. I set the alarm for 5:30 a.m., knowing the helicopter would be arriving at the resort at 6:00 a.m. I wanted to get out there early to meet it. I got into bed and, trying not to think of Talia out in the elements—hurt, cold, starving, dehydrated, and totally scared—fell asleep in my dry, somewhat warm room and bed. *I should be the one outside,* I thought. I would have done anything to be with Talia.

CHAPTER THREE

DECEMBER 25

The alarm went off, and as soon as I woke up
I wanted to cry. It was pouring outside, and
stormy, dark, and windy. There was no way the helicopter was
coming at 6:00 a.m.—we had been told it would come if the weather
was nice. *What are we going to do?*

I got dressed, grabbed my backpack with the polo shirts, protein
bars, and water, and headed down the outdoor hallway to get Peter.
We had planned the night before to meet the helicopter together.
I knocked on his door, and we left for the hotel's driving range, in
a pasture area where we had been told the helicopter would land.

We walked down the driveway past some horses and headed
toward the sheltered part of the driving range. I was so scared
the helicopter wasn't going to come and that no one was going to
be out there looking for Talia, again, for the third day—that any
hope of finding her and Michael and Frankie alive was dwindling.
And I was really scared that Talia was alone and suffering while
she waited for me to come for her.

Throughout the last two days I had been pretty good about holding back my tears, but now, waiting with Peter for a helicopter that might not be coming at all, I broke down. This was the kind of thing that happened in the movies—not to me. Never in a million years would I have imagined getting a call that my daughter's plane was missing, and then have absolutely no ability to find it. This wasn't something you could plan for, something you could possibly know how to deal with. The only thing that could have kept me sane was to get out there and do something, but the weather was making it impossible. It had been this way since we arrived in Boquete, and it was not letting up.

After waiting with Peter for almost an hour under cover, we saw Sam pull up in the driveway near the registration area. The rain had let up a bit, but the clouds were still thick and, not knowing when—or if—the helicopter would arrive, we walked back to the hotel to meet the rest of the Lewises and grab a quick breakfast. I didn't know where Bob, Linda, and Jim were. They hadn't called me since the night before, when I had spoken to Bob about the ex-Seals.

While we were in the restaurant, the helicopter did land at the resort. The pilot came into the restaurant to grab some food while waiting for the weather to improve. Although he would have flown in inclement weather himself, he wasn't willing to take Peter or me up until the weather cleared.

We ordered eggs and pancakes, but I was unable to eat. My daughter was still missing! I was going into shock, and I couldn't speak. All I could do at this point was to keep talking to Talia in my head, hoping she would somehow hear my voice telepathically, telling her to keep holding on, to stay strong, until we somehow got to her.

Finally, the weather cleared a bit, and the helicopter was able to take off. But for some strange reason the pilot had landed in a small area among trees and couldn't take off from there with passengers. He had to take off by himself and fly to a larger takeoff and landing pad where there would be sufficient room to lift off with passengers. So we all got into Sam's Suburban and drove out of the resort, trying to follow the helicopter.

It was going too fast for us to keep up, and then it went behind a hill and completely disappeared into the clouds. It was heading out of Boquete! We stayed on the road, and Sam called a man who was in radio contact with the pilot. The pilot told the man, who in turn told Sam, that he was going to land at the stadium down the road. At last we would get to start looking!

When we got to the stadium, not only was the helicopter not there yet, but the gate was locked. How were we going to get in with the only entrance padlocked? Sam seemed to know everyone in town, and he called a friend of his who knew someone who would come with the key to open the gate. *Great, but when?*

After we sat outside the stadium gate for about half an hour, a man finally arrived with the key. In the meantime, the helicopter had landed on the field inside. I figured once we got into the stadium, Peter and I would hop into the helicopter and we would take off. Wrong again. Though the weather at the stadium seemed clear enough to fly, the pilot told us the weather closer to the mountain was not flyable. I was going to scream!

Meanwhile, my phone had not stopped ringing all morning. It was now about 9:00 a.m., and I had been answering it every minute since 7:00 a.m. Reporters, family, friends and acquaintances from home, friends of Michael—it was non-stop. Many of our friends were trying to get us planes, helicopters, military support, everything we needed—only none of it was coming through! It wasn't these people's fault; it was a political mess. Bob and Linda never called that morning.

I noticed the stadium bleachers were filling up with people. I had no idea who these people were—nobody spoke English. It seemed they were locals coming out to see what was going on. People started taking pictures of us standing there in shock. A camera crew showed up. I think they were there to watch the tragedy unfold. It was crazy.

My phone kept ringing off the hook. My battery was dying again, and I needed to find an outlet. A nice woman—I think she was the girlfriend of one of the reporters—offered to let me sit in her car to charge my phone. I accepted. I had to have power!

It was unreal. Here I was in Panama, in some strange little town, in some strange woman's car, charging my phone, while waiting to get into a small, old, private helicopter to go up in a storm to look for my daughter, missing with her dad and friend in a small plane in the mountains. There was no controlling my crying at this point. In fact, all control had disappeared. It was incredibly hard not knowing.

Finally the pilot waved that it was OK to fly. *Thank God!* I was going to get in this helicopter and find my daughter. In I got. In Peter got. On went our seat belts. We put on the headsets and the pilot started the motor. Only Peter's headset worked, however; I couldn't hear a thing, so I had no idea what the pilot was saying. It probably didn't matter because he didn't speak English and I didn't speak Spanish, but it would have been nice just to be able to hear his voice.

Up we went. I wasn't scared for myself at all, but I was incredibly distraught that I hadn't heard any news from Bob or anyone from the Boquete search and rescue office saying they had found the plane and everyone was OK.

We flew west. I stared down from the helicopter windows at nothing but green. Until this moment I really had no idea how dense the jungle was. The scenery was monotonous. All I saw were steep sides of the mountains, steep canyons, tall peaks—all intensely dense and green. No sign of the plane anywhere.

After about fifteen minutes, the pilot turned around and started back to the stadium. *What's happening?* I had no idea why we were heading back so soon because I couldn't hear a thing. It wasn't until we landed back at the stadium and the motor was turned off that I found out the weather was so bad where we were heading that we had to turn back. *F**k! Nothing is going right! Where is my daughter!*

By the time I got out of the helicopter I was angry, scared, in shock. I felt as if I were in a time warp. I wasn't aware of much; all I knew was that I had to get to the Boquete headquarters and find out what was going on. I had heard *nothing* from anyone about anything.

I looked around and saw a couple of the Boquete search volunteers pulling out in their truck from the parking lot next to the field where we had landed. I ran up to them and asked in broken Spanish where they were going; they said they were going to the headquarters. I understood this much because they said "SINAPROC," which was the name of the search and rescue headquarters. *Thank God!* I asked if they would take me too, and of course they said yes. At no other time in my life have I gotten into a car with complete strangers, but I didn't think twice; I had to get going, and I had to find my daughter.

When we pulled up at the search and rescue headquarters, I jumped out and went in. Valerie and Kirk were there, looking at the big map on the wall; moments later Linda and Jim showed up. Bob had apparently left early that morning with one of the search groups heading up the mountain on foot. He's a hiker and runner in great physical shape, so he was totally capable of going up the mountain.

I don't remember what time it was—I think it was late morning. But despite the fact that some people were now searching by foot, there didn't seem to be much going on. I couldn't take it any longer. I told the main man in the office to tell everyone possible that there was now a reward, a $25,000 reward, which would go to the first person or people who found that plane and my daughter.

As soon as he heard this, he immediately got on the telephone and told someone in Spanish about the reward. Then he told the other people in the office, and they all got on their cell phones and called more people, and finally things began to happen. People started to show up within minutes, wanting to participate in the search. We went from having just a few groups of searchers to having many more people.

Another volunteer, possibly the wife or girlfriend of one of the men in charge, arrived. Within minutes she was on the radio making an announcement that went out over Panamanian radio about the missing plane, the people on the plane—and the reward. *Finally something is going to happen! Finally we have people coming out to help search!*

The weather was still bad, and the search and rescue office didn't have much gear for the searchers to take. All these men were going out in jeans and non-waterproof shoes, with not much more than a backpack, a machete, and some plastic trash bags—their only rain gear.

Sam came into the office at this point, and Bob returned from the search. Kirk and Peter were there, along with Jim and Linda, and together we all stared at the map while Sam showed us where more sightings had occurred and where the searchers were. It seemed all the sightings had been in one area, which made it possible to narrow down the search to a more specific area in the southwestern portion of the mountains.

We felt certain that the plane had made an emergency landing in a giant riverbed area or in the farmland around one of the big crevasses. Wherever it was, I was starting to feel hopeful that we would soon find the plane and get there to find Talia sitting inside, out of the rain, waiting for me, her mom, whom she knew would show up, no matter what.

Bob headed out on another search. I plugged my phone into the outlet between the desk and the coffeemaker and sat squished in the corner, watching men come in and out of the office. I was so thankful for all of these men—and so angry that I had been stopped from offering the reward the day before.

My cell phone never stopped ringing. I had to squat down in my little spot and talk with my face in my lap because my charger cord was too short. The phone never had a chance to ring out loud because I would get an incoming call while I was on the phone. I had to answer every call. Each time I thought it would be Talia, calling from the strange house of some helpful person who had found her and the others. I was not going to miss that call.

But it was never Talia. It was either a reporter or a friend from home, asking how it was going, or another person offering to help somehow.

One call that held out some hope was from a salesman, Kurt, who worked for Michael at his investment firm, Pacificor. He said he was on another line with the CEO of Global Rescue, a company that had access to helicopters and experienced search and rescue personnel. The CEO wanted to talk to me, and Kurt conferenced me in.

The CEO began by telling me about his company, which I really didn't need to hear, and then asked me what I needed. I was very clear: I needed Black Hawk helicopters, or other weather-resistant helicopters, and men to rappel out of them to search the jungle. I told him I needed them now, not tomorrow but ASAP. I said these men and helicopters must have night vision and infrared sensing capability. I could not have been clearer.

The CEO asked, *if* he could get this stuff, would I want it. I had just told him, "Get me this stuff *now*"—what was the *if? If you can do it, then prove it and get me the supplies!* Honestly, the guy seemed more like a marketer than someone capable of getting anything done.

I said, "If you can get me the men and equipment I need, and have it here ASAP, then tell Kurt to work it out; just get it to me quick." I had done all I could do; now it was up to Kurt to seal the deal. But it didn't pan out. Like so many others, they acted as if they could save the world—but they couldn't deliver. All this call did was get me excited about help that would never come.

I had no idea where anyone was. The office was quiet again, since all the new men who had come out to search had headed into the mountains.

I had to get out of that office for some air. With phone and charger in hand, I went outside and noticed a little shop across the street called The Shalom Bakery. Now, that was strange. Shalom Bakery in Panama! I headed over for a bagel and some water, and when I walked in, there were Valerie and Rosie, Linda and Catalina.

I looked around for an outlet, as I did every time I went into any building whatsoever, and found one. Under the bar. I plugged my phone in, ordered a bagel, and sat down. We all were speechless. Really, we had nothing to say. What was there to say? We were in shock. Our daughters were still missing.

Michael was missing. It was now forty-eight hours since the plane had gone missing.

We had been sitting in that shop for quite awhile when suddenly we saw a bunch of men running out of the search office with their backpacks. They started jumping into their vehicles and taking off. We knew they must have found them because one of the guys grabbed a stretcher before jumping into the back of one of the trucks. We ran outside and were able to stop one of the cars as it was driving off.

"What's going on? Did you find them? Did you find them?" We were frantic.

One of the men inside the car held up one finger, his index finger, and said, "One."

One what? One person was found? Which person was found, and where? Who found them, and where are the others? All these questions—and no answers! They drove off and left us standing in the street, not knowing anything.

At this point my brain ceased to function. I went into a kind of daze, thinking to myself over and over, *Please, God, let it be Talia, please, it has to be, it cannot be any other way, they have to have found Talia safe and sound.*

A man came out of the office while we were standing on the walkway near the door. He told us that the one person found was a girl. Oh, my God, I was about to die—*which girl?* He told us he didn't know which girl, but that she was found walking through the jungle far from the plane with hypothermia and a broken arm. The others had not been found yet.

What was she doing walking through the jungle? How did she get there? Where are the others? All I could imagine was that the others had broken legs and this girl did not, so she had taken off to find help. I couldn't imagine any other scenario.

Time came to a complete standstill. I have no idea how much time passed, but as I continued thinking about why the one girl was walking alone, a man pulled up and said he knew the name of the girl who had been found. Oh, my God, I was about to throw up and pass out. Valerie and I were standing on the walkway between the street and the porch of the little office, staring at each other, both of us praying to hear our daughter's name. I could hardly bear it, but on the outside I was as still as could be. Valerie and I continued to look at each other as the man told us the name of the girl. It was Frankie.

My heart sank. I was happy for Val, but I wasn't going to believe that just because Frankie was the one they had found, Talia was anything but fine. There had to be a reason Frankie was far from the plane, alone, and it had nothing to do with Talia not being OK. I did let myself think that Talia might be hurt—if she were not hurt, she would have been walking with Frankie—but hurt was OK because she was still there waiting for me.

Again, I have no idea how much time passed, but Bob came back from his search and told me he heard they had found Frankie. I told him, "Yes, we don't know why they were separated, but Frankie was walking around away from the plane."

I vaguely remember Peter coming up the walkway towards me, but nothing else. I would later learn that he was the one who told me they had found the others, but none had survived. But when he told me how sorry he was that Talia and Michael had not made it, I just stared at him blankly, as if in a coma. Nothing registered, and he knew that I was barely conscious. He hugged me, kissed my head, and left me alone. All I remember is hearing they had found Frankie walking and wondering why.

I heard many stories that day about how they found Frankie, how they found the plane, how they found Talia and Michael.

None of them had any basis in reality for me; I simply knew they weren't true. I knew that another call would come in, saying they had made it to the plane and Talia was there with her dad, a little hurt but still OK.

One of the stories was that the plane crashed and Frankie was thrown from the plane. If that was the case, then Talia and Michael were still in the plane but could not jump down that far, so Frankie had gone to get help. *Don't tell me that Talia is dead. Not true. She just cannot get out by herself.*

Then someone said the plane had burst into flames and burned, and the others were in the burned plane. *How is that possible? We would have seen the smoke. How did Frankie get out? If Frankie got thrown before the fire, then so did Talia, so we have to keep looking.*

Then we were told that there was no fire, but the plane was stuck in the trees. *If that's the case, how do we know that Talia and Michael are not alive but unconscious and in need of medical attention, and are being forgotten because of the false belief that they're dead?*

Then we were told that the rescuers had climbed up the tree and made sure they were dead.

How did they do this? They didn't have equipment for climbing. This can't be true.

I didn't believe any of these stories. They were wrong, all of them.

Then suddenly, I was no longer sure about anything. I knew I could believe Peter, but I couldn't remember what he had told me earlier. I do remember seeing Bob and telling him they needed to send someone up there to get Talia and Michael. I remember telling him they could be unconscious, that the untrained Panamanian men might think they were dead when they really were not.

All this time, my phone continued to ring. As soon as I had heard about the possible fire, I had freaked out and called J. He asked if I wanted them to come now, and I said not yet. I knew the stories weren't true; I knew Talia was going to come back any time.

When I hung up from my call with him, my phone immediately rang. I remember this phone call very clearly. I was on the steps of the Boquete search and rescue office, and I answered my phone. It was Susan Armstrong from the U.S. Embassy.

"Hi, Kim, this is Susan Armstrong. I want to express my deepest condolences for your loss." *Loss, what loss are you talking about?* I was pissed. *Don't you think it's premature to express your condolences? No one is dead; just because they found one girl doesn't mean the others are dead.* I hung up on her.

What I did not know was that the men who had found the plane, Miguel and Manuel Burac, had indeed verified that Frankie was the sole survivor. They had contacted the head of the Panamanian search and rescue in Panama City, who had called the U.S. Embassy, and Susan Armstrong had already spoken to my brother by the time I called him to tell him about the rumor of the fire. J. had not been able to get the words out of his mouth to tell me Talia was dead. I had hung up after telling him not to come yet, not knowing the truth. When Susan called me, she indeed had the facts. I did not.

I still didn't believe it. I wasn't going to until I was given the whole story. So far, the story was not real. There were too many versions. All we knew for sure was that they had found Frankie. The rest had not been verified to me.

I'm not sure at what point I accepted the truth about Talia and Michael. I must have known by the time I called my brother again to tell him it was time for him and our parents to come to Panama, but I don't even remember calling him. Of course, by the time I called, they already knew and were trying to book their flights.

(Luckily, J. was able to make reservations for himself and my parents on a Copa flight that night—the same flight Bob's wife, Lynne, and a friend of theirs, Jim W., ended up on. I say luckily, because two attempts by Michael's pilot and another friend to provide a private jet to bring them all down fell through. Ironically, like her husband just days before, Lynne had not contacted my family about coming down together.)

It was getting dark, so Linda, the Lewises, and I went back to Sam's hotel and went to our rooms, in shock. Linda and Catalina, Valerie and Rosie came to my room. The hotel didn't normally have room service, but Sam had told us to order it and he would make sure we got it.

We ordered sandwiches, salads and drinks. I lay down on my bed next to Valerie and started to cry. Linda came in and lay down next to me too, and we all cried. My phone kept ringing. I didn't know whom all the calls were from. I just knew that I would never be the same again. Ever.

After I learned that Talia did not survive the crash—or, more specifically, after I fully realized it—I had absolutely no memory of our life together at all. I couldn't remember a single thing! Not her smell, her touch, or anything we had ever talked about. It was a horrible feeling. It was as if someone had erased my entire memory bank. I was so afraid I would never remember anything about her or us together. But I couldn't focus on remembering. All I could think about was how I was going to live without Talia. How on earth was I going to make it through the rest of my life?

At some point Jim came to my room and told Linda it was time to go home—Catalina was tired. Linda asked me if I wanted to stay at the hotel or come home to her house. I didn't know what to do.

What was going through my head was this: *Do I stay at the hotel, in a room all by myself, and cry alone all night, or go to Linda's house and be with "family" that really doesn't care about me at all.* Which was worse? I debated for a couple of minutes. I could tell that Valerie knew what I was thinking. She had witnessed the coldness of the Kleins and knew I was struggling with this choice.

I decided to go to Linda's. Not because it was the better choice for me, but because I knew if I didn't go, I would be out of the loop. Jim was getting the real facts about the search, but I wouldn't be called. So I went, out of the need for information and for the sake of self-preservation.

I grabbed my backpack and stuffed my clothes in it. For some strange reason I thought I would be back the next day, so I left my bag of overpriced phone plugs in the room and headed out. But that would be the last time I was in that room, and the last time I was with the Lewises on this life path. They would be bringing their daughter home on the plane alive, sitting next to them; I was now the mother of a dead girl, taking her home in a box.

We all squished into Jim's car—Jim, Linda, Catalina, Bob, and I—and headed back down the mountain to David. I don't remember the ride. When we got to Linda's we all separated for a while. Linda showed me how the water worked in the bathroom so I could shower. Basically, it didn't work—the water was just a dribble. But at least there was some water. So I took a quick shower and put on one of the clean shirts I had bought at Sam's resort. Then I lay down and started to cry into my towel.

All night I heard various people crying. I covered my face with my arm to block out the light. The next thing I knew, I woke up and saw Linda in the living room, where I had fallen asleep.

CHAPTER FOUR

DECEMBER 26

I lay in bed, not wanting to get up, not wanting to deal with this new day. Linda came over. She told me she and her dad had been talking the night before, and they knew I was probably stressed over money. She said I didn't need to be concerned, that she and Bob would take care of me.

The thought of money had not entered my mind. All I really cared about was how I was going to live without Talia in my life. But it was nice of her. Little did I know that she and Bob didn't mean a word of it.

I knew it would not be too long before my family arrived. *Thank God.*

I got dressed, and we all headed back up to Boquete. We had to find out where the bodies were and when we could see them. We weren't even sure whether the rescuers had gotten Frankie off the mountain.

At the search headquarters, we learned that most of the stories we had been told were not true. Frankie had been found trapped in the plane, strapped in, face down. The suitcases had fallen on her. Talia was in the plane, but it was unclear whether Frankie could see her. Michael and the pilot had been found outside the plane.

We learned that the rescue team had not been able to get Frankie down the mountain the day before. By the time they reached the plane, hours after it had been found by the Burac brothers, it was nearly dark. It took a long time to free Frankie from the wreckage, and they had to evaluate her condition before moving her out of the plane.

She was in very bad condition. She was weak and dehydrated, suffering from hypothermia, and could barely speak. She also had what looked like a broken arm, a broken nose, and other wounds. Because of her condition, as well as the harshness of the weather and the terrain, Frankie and the rescuers remained on the mountain all night. It took four men to carry her down the mountain on a stretcher the next morning. The jungle was very steep and covered in deep, sticky mud. It also took four additional men to cut a path through the vines and trees to get her and Talia's and Michael's bodies down the mountain.

Bob and I were told that if we went to the stadium and waited, the helicopter that was going to transport Frankie to the hospital would pick us up and take us up the mountain to Talia and Michael. At last I would go up there and see for myself what had happened, and be there to keep Talia's body safe.

We waited patiently at the field. We heard a helicopter but couldn't see it. Then we heard it pass us. Where was it going? One of the Panamanians with us told us the helicopter had Frankie and was going directly to the hospital. But what about Talia and Michael?

Someone told us another helicopter would soon be landing at the stadium to take Bob and me up the mountain. Then we found out that the inspectors had to go up in that helicopter, and there wasn't enough room for both of us to go with them. Bob insisted that he should go because he was a doctor. He needed to see for himself if they were really dead. I had no objection to that.

But when the second helicopter finally landed at the field, Bob wasn't allowed on it. Only the inspectors could go. There wasn't enough room on this flight, period. They told us not to worry, saying that as soon as the inspectors were dropped off on the mountain, the helicopter would come back and pick up Bob—and me, too, if I wanted to go—and take us up to the landing site.

Again there was a snag. The landing site was a three-hour hike from the crash site—a very strenuous three hours. I didn't think I could make this hike, but Bob could. I had to decide whether I was going to try. I didn't know what to do. I had to be with Talia; I couldn't go on any longer without her. I couldn't stand it.

Just as I decided I would go home with Linda and wait, the option to go was taken away from Bob. We were told there was no use in him going because Talia and Michael had to stay up on the mountain until the crash inspectors were able to get up to the site and do a full investigation of the crash. This inspection would take a number of hours, if not all night.

I freaked out again. My poor daughter was lying up there and had to stay on the mountain until the Panamanian government said it was OK to move her! None of us were happy with this, but we had no choice.

Then it got worse. The inspectors took off in the helicopter, and a few minutes later we heard that it wasn't able to land due to bad weather. Could anything go right for us?

What we did have was the ability to make sure nothing happened to Talia's and Michael's bodies. Now that the site had been found, people might try to get up there and take photos, which would have been horrifying to me, and steal their things. We were truly afraid their bodies and belongings would be disturbed or stolen. Jim, with Sam's help, I believe, arranged to have a large number of Panamanian Indians go up the mountain and stay with the bodies, guarding them until the inspectors had completed their work and would allow Talia and Michael to be taken off the mountain.

At this point we were all helpless. We got in the car and headed down the mountain back to David. It would be hours before our family members landed at the David airport, so we went back to Linda's to rest a bit.

As soon as we got to Linda's, I lay down on the couch, which was my bed, and cried. I then drifted into a half-sleep. Just as I was drifting off, I had a strange feeling on my wrist. It was as if someone had wrapped their fingers around my left wrist. Just for a moment, then it was gone. I opened my eyes. *Talia, was that you? I know it's you. I love you, Sugar, so much!* I just knew it was Talia touching me—she was trying to communicate with me!

Minutes later, a friend of mine called. She told me she had just gotten off the phone with Rebecca, a spirit communicator I had seen in the past. It seems my friend—distraught that Rebecca had not foreseen the accident and stopped me from sending Talia on the trip that ultimately killed her—had called Rebecca to let her know about the accident and to express her anger. During that conversation, Rebecca started to get messages from Talia that were meant for me.

I realized that this conversation between Rebecca and my friend had happened at the same time I felt the pressure on my wrist, Talia's touch. As my friend and Rebecca spoke, Talia showed Rebecca something. Rebecca wasn't sure exactly what Talia was holding out to her, but she knew it was gold and small. *Like a charm or something.* Talia told Rebecca she wanted me to take that item from her body.

When my friend told me this, I knew right then that it was Talia's bracelet. Talia had touched my arm to tell me to take her bracelet from her wrist—the one I had given her on the last Mother's Day. I had given it to her as a thank-you gift. Thanking her for being my daughter. The bracelet was very simple, just a small gold coin on a black rope. This bracelet meant a great deal to both Talia and me. It was Talia's absolute favorite thing in the world; she had told me so. She never took it off, ever.

As soon as my friend and I hung up, Rebecca called me herself. She was excited because Talia had gotten through to her again. Through that communication Talia clarified what she had been trying to tell me. It *was* her bracelet she wanted me to get. I knew it!

Gradually, people started to come out of their little areas of the house. We decided to go and eat before we went to the airport to pick up our families. I had no appetite, but I ate a little soup. After lunch we went to the David airport to wait for the commuter flight from Panama City.

When we got to the airport, it was a sit-and-wait situation. Though my parents had been on the flight to Panama City with Lynne and Jim W., they were coming in on a different commuter flight from David. I really hoped my parents would get in first, because I knew once Lynne and Jim W. arrived, I would be left alone. And that's just about what happened.

When Lynne's plane came in, Bob greeted her and Jim W. Then he told me he was going to leave. I either asked him to wait for my family's plane or said it would be nice if they waited with me—I don't recall. It wasn't that it was dangerous or that I couldn't handle it, but I was waiting for my family to come because my daughter was *dead*. I didn't want to be left alone. Bob stayed, though it was clear that he didn't want to.

Fortunately, we had only a few minutes to wait. Once the plane landed and my family walked through the gate to the reception area, I totally broke down. I couldn't help it. I first cried with my mom, then with my dad, then with my brother. It was terrible. I can't even describe how sad this was.

My mom went up to Bob to hug him. He was distant and gave her a fake hug. He's never really nice; there's never any real emotion.

Jose, one of the drivers for the Secas, was waiting to drive my family and me to the Hotel Nacionale in David, where Linda's ex-husband, Doug, had made reservations for us. We were all about to go our separate ways.

Before leaving, I asked Linda and Jim to please call me when they had some news about Talia and Michael, no matter what. I wasn't happy that they were still up on the mountain, but at least we knew where they were. And the Indians were watching over them. These Indians are very spiritual, and I knew they would protect Talia's and Michael's bodies.

In the meantime, the family of the pilot had somehow sneaked up the mountain and carried his body away. It was against the law, because the inspection had not occurred yet, but they did it anyway. I knew how they felt, wanting their loved one off the mountain.

Jose drove us to the hotel and gave me his phone number so I could call him if we needed to go anywhere. Here we were, at some strange hotel in Panama, together as a family for the first time in years. But we were not a family. We were without Talia.

After we checked in, we decided to go downstairs to have dinner. As we walked into the hotel restaurant, the TV in the place was broadcasting a news story about the missing plane and how Talia and Michael had been found dead. It was strange—I didn't really feel any emotion because I couldn't relate to the story at all. It was as if I were watching someone else's life, not my own. I just sat there, watching and listening, staring in a trance. Everyone in the restaurant knew who we were. They knew I was the dead girl's mom, and they all looked at me with sad faces, saying nothing.

We ordered, ate a bit, went to our rooms, and got ready for bed. Tomorrow was going to be a bad day. It was the day we would bring Talia and Michael down off the mountain, the day I would take the lifeless bodies of my daughter and her father to the morgue.

At this point I felt an intense desire to call Rebecca. Talia wanted to talk to me; I needed to hear from Talia, to connect with my daughter somehow. I needed to hear whatever she had to say.

I left a message for Rebecca, then lay on the bed, trying to sleep. But my mind was racing. *How did this happen? What happened? How could this be?* Then the phone rang. It was Rebecca.

She relayed to me some things that Talia wanted me to know.

Talia said she loved me. She said she was with her dad and that she and Michael had stayed with Frankie and kept her in a daze until she was found, in order to keep her from panicking and to keep her safe. Talia said she and Michael had protected Frankie.

Talia repeated that she wanted me to get her bracelet, and she wanted me to get her backpack. She was concerned about her dogs and her horses. Talia said she wanted to make sure I collected all her riding awards. Then she said tomorrow was going to be a very hard day for me and, most important, not to look at her this way. She was talking about the fact that I was going to see her lifeless, and she didn't want me to remember her like that.

Talia also said that she had had a perfect, charmed life with me, the best life. She said I was the best mom, and that I would always be her mom.

Rebecca said Michael asked me not to be mad at him. He thanked me for being such a great mom to Talia. He also said he had guided Sam to help with the search.

Talia and Michael said a lot more, but these were the most important things to me at the time.

Finally I fell asleep. I don't know what time it was, but it was probably 3:00 a.m.

CHAPTER FIVE

DECEMBER 27

I woke up around 7:00 a.m. and got dressed. I wanted to go to the hospital to see Frankie. I wanted to see how she was doing and find out what had happened. I wasn't sure I would be allowed to see her or talk to her, but I had to try.

My parents wanted to go with me, so we grabbed a cab to the hospital in David, just five minutes away from the hotel.

We went to Frankie's room and found her parents and uncle talking outside. Frankie was asleep. We weren't allowed to see her, but Valerie and the others filled me in on how she was doing. They said Frankie didn't remember much at all, but she kept saying she had been in and out of sleep the whole time she was up there, in a daze. That's what Talia had said to me via Rebecca—she had kept Frankie in a daze to keep her safe. Frankie said she would dream of home, then talk to Michael and Talia, then go back to sleep. We knew she wasn't really talking to Talia and Michael; Talia and Michael had been killed instantly.

It was very hard for me not knowing what had happened up there, but this wasn't the time to find out. Frankie was asleep, and besides, I didn't want to ask her anything that might hurt her recovery or mess with her memory and emotions.

Just as I finished talking to Valerie and Kirk, Jim came over. He had stopped by to see how Frankie was. He also wanted to warn the Lewises that there was a media frenzy and *not* to talk to the media. Reporters were coming up to anyone they thought was family, despite Jim telling them to stay away. Bob, Jim, and I all thought the Lewises had agreed that talking to the media was a bad idea, but we later found out they had been talking to the TV program *20/20* at the hospital.

When Jim turned to leave, I told him we were going with him. He looked surprised and a bit disturbed but didn't tell us we couldn't. It was a good thing: I needed to be where the information was, and the Panamanian government was in contact with Jim because he was the local man and spoke Spanish. I was not going to be forgotten and left out of decisions that had to be made about my daughter. So we all squished into Jim's truck and headed over to Linda's house to join Bob, Lynne, Jim W., and Doug.

We sat around waiting for the call that would notify us that the investigation at the crash site was finished, and the bodies could be carried down the mountain and brought to the morgue in David by helicopter. But it was not still. My phone was ringing off the hook. Calls from the CEO of Copa, Joseph P., who was helping me arrange all our flights home. Calls from friends and media. Calls from other Panamanian officials we had contacted to help us have Talia and Michael released to come home.

Jim W. was off meeting with the forensic doctor. He was trying to get her to agree to stay late and do the government-mandated autopsies immediately so that we could leave Panama as soon as possible. I have no idea how he did it, but somehow he was able to convince her to work into the night until the autopsies were finished. We didn't want autopsies at all, but the Panamanian government required them and would not let us take the bodies back to the U.S. without them.

One of the calls that came in on my phone was from Michael's mother, Anne. She was hysterical. She was in Vietnam on vacation, and it seemed no one had called her to tell her about her son and granddaughter. Anne found out because friends she was traveling with heard about the plane crash on the news and went to her room to tell her.

I felt terribly sorry for her. When I first arrived in Panama, I asked Linda if she had called her mom. She said she had e-mailed her, leading me to believe that Anne was aware of the situation and that they were actually corresponding. Not the case. Anne had not gotten the e-mail—and no one had even tried to call her. I would have called her, but Linda had been clear that Anne already knew.

Besides being overwhelmed by the news, Anne was furious. She asked me about the crash, and I told her all I knew. Which really wasn't much. I then told her she should talk to Bob. I gave him my phone, and he spoke with her himself. It was a very difficult call.

In the meantime, Jim got a call from someone who said paparazzi had overrun the airport where the helicopter carrying Talia and Michael was expected to land. Michael was a superstar in Panama and all over the world. This was a big story. So Jim decided to go down to the airport and get everyone under control before the helicopter came.

Finally, after a few hours on the phone, trying to move mountains, we got a call. Not only was the investigation at the crash site complete, and Talia and Michael could now be moved, but the President of Panama was sending his personal helicopter to pick up their bodies. Here he was, sending his personal helicopter now, while the media was watching—when throughout the search he had done nothing to help. *Nothing at all.* Well, at least we had a helicopter.

The next call was from someone at the helicopter landing pad, which was just a small clearing on the mountainside, telling us that the men moving Talia and Michael down the mountain had reached the pad, and they were preparing to take off for David.

Jim called from the airport, saying it was a madhouse. He told Bob that only he should go to the morgue to identify the bodies. Bob repeated this to me. What, did they think it was enough to have Bob see Talia? No way on earth was I not going to see Talia. Not only were they nuts for thinking this, but selfish and cruel.

I said, "No way, I'm going and so are my parents." An argument erupted. Bob and Lynne said there were too many people and no one should go. I said, "This is my daughter, and I'll take my family if I want. I should not be in Panama talking about my dead daughter, and what's more, I should not have to fight for the right to see her for the last time."

Lynne decided to butt in. She came up to me and said I needed to do what was best for the whole. *The whole what?* I lost it. I told her, "I don't give a shit about the whole, I care about my daughter. She is *my daughter,* and I'm going, and I'm taking whoever I want with me!"

There were so many people standing in the driveway with us that it was pandemonium. I realized my parents couldn't go with me to see Talia; the taxi was too small to hold us all. I decided to take just my brother. I needed his support, but I didn't need everyone. J., Bob, and I got into a taxi and headed off to the morgue. It was not that far—nothing in David is that far from anything else—but the ride seemed to last an eternity. Here I was in a Panamanian taxi, trying to tell the driver where to take us in Spanish, a language I don't speak. I told him to take us to the house of the dead—that was all I could figure out to say. But he got it, and drove us to the correct place.

When we got to the morgue, there was so much security that the media were kept pretty far from the entrance. We pulled in just as the truck that held Talia and Michael was backing up to get as close to the door as possible. We parked; I jumped out and went over to the side of the truck. The media were snapping photos with really long lenses, so we tried to stand with our backs toward them to block their view of the bodies. My heart was racing. Any second, the truck doors would open and Talia would be carried out. My poor little daughter, dead.

The truck doors opened, and slowly one body was moved out. The bodies were wrapped and covered, but I could tell which was Talia and which was Michael by the size.

Once they were taken into the morgue, we went into the front office and just stood there, waiting for the doctor to prepare the bodies before we could see them. Bob again told me he thought he should be the only one to go in. He said that since he was a doctor, he was used to seeing bodies, and though it was going to be very hard for him to see Talia and Michael, he was better prepared than I was.

Again I told him there was no way I was not going to see Talia. Bob was concerned that I would see her in a state I didn't want to remember her in. I told him I could do it but decided to let him go first, just to verify.

That discussion was not necessary. The doctor came out and told us the bodies were in good enough condition; we didn't have to worry about seeing anything too bad. Now we had to sit and wait until we were allowed to see them.

The little office filled up with people. The crash inspectors came in; a woman who said she was a judge came in. They all needed to get information about Talia and Michael—their birthdays, our names, and other information. Finally, the doctor came out and said we could go in.

As soon as I walked in and could see around the corner, I saw Talia. I also saw Michael. They were each lying on a table, still.

I went up to Talia. She was naked, but wrapped in a paper covering of some sort, with a blanket over that. The first thing I remember was Bob coming over to me, asking if the bracelet Talia was wearing was the one I wanted to get. Yes, it was *the* bracelet. I was so grateful she had it on her still and it had not been lost or stolen. Bob helped me remove it from Talia's cold, moist wrist. Her little hands. Her fingers. Her wrist. Cold. I got the bracelet and put it on my own wrist, then moved closer to talk to her.

Talia's face was not harmed, but it had a look of *Oh, my God.* Definitely not a happy or peaceful look, but a shocked look. A concerned look. I read her look and felt she had been thinking, *Mommy! I'm scared!* I can see her face now. I will never, ever be free of that expression.

Talia's hair was wet and limp. Her eyes were shut, her body wet and cold. I leaned down and hugged her, and I kissed her and started talking to her. I told her how much I loved her. I told her that I knew how much she loved me, that I missed her, that I had had the best life because of her, that she was the best thing in my life, that I was grateful for every second I had had with her. I couldn't let her go. I couldn't stop hugging her. I had to, though, because the doctor told me she had to proceed.

I left Talia and went to Michael. I had to say goodbye to him too. I looked at his face; unlike Talia's, it was expressionless. I told Michael to take care of Talia. I told him I forgave him for treating me so badly all these years, but he had to make sure Talia was OK in heaven. Then I went back to Talia. The doctor told me I had to go, but I asked her for one more minute. I couldn't go, I couldn't leave Talia. I wanted to stay with her forever. If I could have died on the spot to be with her, I would have.

I hugged her and kissed her goodbye. *I love you.* The last hug and kiss I could give her. Then I walked out of that room, back into the office. That was my last time with Talia in her physical form.

The office was full of people. My parents and Jim were there. I told them Talia was OK. I was not, but I held myself together; I still had to do some sort of paperwork.

The judge called me into another room to answer questions. An interpreter was there. I don't really remember the questions, other than the simple ones. *Is that your daughter? Did you recognize her? What is her birthday? When is your birthday? Is this her passport number?* Just official questions. Then I left the room while Bob went in to answer the same questions about Michael.

We were done. The doctor was left alone with Talia and Michael. She was going to start on the autopsies, working overtime so the bodies could be transported to the morgue in Panama City overnight and cremated in the morning. The U.S. Embassy required that we take Talia and Michael to a special approved morgue there for cremation. I was notified of all this at the last minute, so I don't even know whether the doctor did a proper autopsy.

Jim W. had worked a miracle by having the autopsies done that night and getting an overnight driver for the six-hour drive to Panama City. He was also the one who arranged to have Talia and Michael cremated the next morning, so we wouldn't have to stay in Panama another day. He said normally we would have been stuck down there for a few weeks; I don't know how he managed to get it all done overnight. He may have paid someone off—I just don't know. All I knew was that I was going back to the hotel with my family and no Talia.

When we got back to the hotel, Bob called and told me we would all be able to get out of David the next afternoon. He said he would book the commuter flights from David to Panama City for my family and me. Finally, he was doing something nice! I told him I had not heard back from Val, the Copa representative that the C.E.O., Joseph P., had put us in contact with, but she was taking care of the flight arrangements from Panama City to America for all of us. We would be going home the next evening.

I had been told that Linda would be getting the tickets for the commuter flights, so I gave her all our official names. A couple of hours later, Bob called and told me he had bought the commuter tickets for himself, Jim W., and Lynne, but not for my family or me. His excuse was that Lynne, who had actually made the arrangements, didn't have our names. But of course I knew differently. And I knew that the real reason Bob hadn't bought us tickets was that he didn't trust us to pay him back.

I now had to scramble to get us on a flight out of David the next afternoon. The problem was, the airlines' ticket desks were closed. I called American Express Travel Service. They couldn't get us tickets. We tried to call Air Panama and Aeroperlas directly; neither one answered. It was strange. In the U.S. reservation numbers are answered twenty-four hours a day. Not here. I started to panic. We had no flight to Panama City. I needed to get there to collect Talia's ashes and complete the necessary paperwork. It was so nice of Bob to leave us hanging.

December 27

Somehow, my brother was able to get us tickets online. I'm not sure how that happened because the website was not accepting ticket purchases, but a miracle occurred and it worked. The funny part was that we were on a flight that left before Bob's and got us into Panama City in plenty of time, so Bob would not be able to ditch us or handle any paperwork about Talia without me.

It was time to pack. We had to prepare to leave the next day.

CHAPTER SIX

DECEMBER 28

Before we flew out, I had to go with Bob to an office in Boquete to pick up Talia's personal belongings and do some paperwork. Valerie had to go there, too, in order to get Frankie's things. I went over to the hospital early in the morning to try to see Frankie before we left.

At first I was afraid to go in. Frankie was awake and sitting up in bed, and I was concerned that if she saw me, Talia's mom, it might trigger some sort of psychological problem in her. I was also afraid I would break down and not be able to control my crying. I managed to go in and say hi, but neither of us could really speak; we both just stared at each other. I realized I had to get out of there, quickly.

I called Jim and asked him to pick up Valerie and me at the hospital instead of the hotel. He came by with Bob. We didn't talk much in the car. When we got to Boquete, Jim had to drive around a bit to find the office, which was in a different building from search headquarters.

This place was a very small two-room office. In one room were a desk, chair and computer, and in the other room just a desk. The personal belongings were in a closet at the back of this room. When I saw Talia's things, I wanted to rip open her backpack to get her iPhone and computer—I knew these two items had been the most important things to her. But although I could see them once the bag was opened, I wasn't allowed to take them out until everything in the bag had been inventoried.

Bob went first. The official went through Michael's belongings, not really inventorying it, just verifying that everything was Michael's. They had his flight bag with the passports in it.

While Bob was going through Michael's things, one of the officials took out his camera and started looking through the digital photos he had taken at the crash site. I couldn't really see over Bob's shoulders, but for one second I caught a glimpse of Talia's face, flashing across the camera screen. I turned away quickly. I hadn't wanted to see her like that, but the damage was done. Now that picture is etched in my brain, and every once in awhile it flashes before me. My daughter's face and hair, as she lay there on the ground.

It was now my turn to go through Talia's things. It went quickly. The officials were asking Bob questions and typing up a report in Spanish, which he had to sign. I thought I'd have to fill out a report as well, but Bob said he had done it for me. I have no idea what they asked or what he answered, but when I asked him if he was sure the report was done, he was short with me and said, "Yes, I did it, you don't have to."

Valerie began the process of going through Frankie's things. Meanwhile, it was time to get back to David and meet up with everyone else so we could make our flights to Panama City. Bob said goodbye to Valerie and headed out, expecting me to follow.

I was blown away—he was planning on leaving Valerie stranded in Boquete!

Valerie was shocked as well. I immediately called Jose and left a message, asking him to send someone to Boquete to pick up Valerie and take her to David. Just then, the officials said they needed copies of Talia's and Michael's passports. There was no copy machine in the office, so they had to go down the street to make copies. Once we got the passports back, we were able to leave. I said a somewhat emotionless goodbye to Valerie, and we headed out.

Bob rode in front with Jim, and I was in the back seat. As we were leaving Boquete, Bob asked me, "Do you think the Lewises would chip in towards the $25,000 reward?" I wanted to scream. What was wrong with him? I felt strongly that Michael's risk-taking behavior and negligence had killed Talia and almost killed Frankie, and Bob wanted the Lewises to pay part of the reward! "*No*," I said, "don't even ask them."

I suddenly remembered that I owed Bob my share of Rodolfo's charter flight. I grabbed $500 in cash from my bag and handed it to him, saying, "Here's my portion of the charter flight." He took it! I couldn't believe it. Michael's estate could easily have covered it, but no, he took it.

There wasn't enough time now to pick up my family and Lynne and Jim W., so we called and asked them to meet us at the David airport. They were already checked in by the time we arrived. We went to the counter and took care of our tickets—finally, we were ready to leave David. Ironically, it turned out that after Bob had caused us such stress by not buying our commuter tickets to Panama City as he said he would, something had gone wrong with his tickets, and he and his group ended up on our flight.

We all boarded the plane and set off for Panama City to pick up Talia's and Michael's ashes. Jim W. had gone ahead in the truck with their bodies the night before. He had decided to stay with them after the autopsies to ensure nothing happened to them and everything went as planned. He had arrived at the U.S. Embassy's official crematorium very early in the morning and, after turning the bodies over to the mortician, had gone to the embassy to get the death certificates and whatever else was required for us to leave Panama.

On the flight to Panama City my father said he felt Michael. He said Michael was in the cockpit, making sure nothing happened to us. He said he heard Michael in his ear, telling him he was sorry. *Well, he should be, for killing my daughter.*

When we landed, I agreed with Bob that only he and I would go to the crematorium to pick up the ashes. We would meet the others at Tocumen International Airport for the flight home, bringing Jim W. with us. My parents and my brother would take all our luggage to the airport. I got upset when I found out Lynne was coming with us to the crematorium. If Bob had told me she was going, I would have brought my family too.

My family collected all the bags and headed for the airport, and we grabbed a taxi. At first the driver had no idea what we were talking about. What crematorium? Where? Somehow I was able to get across to him where we needed to go. In the discussion it came out that we were going to get Talia's and Michael's ashes, and all of a sudden the driver said, "Wow, I know Mr. Michael. I worked for him; I drove for him and his guests at the Secas!" He said he was good friends with Diego, meaning Doug, Linda's ex-husband. It was strange—of all the taxi drivers we could have found, this one knew Michael.

Bob and Lynne were now saying we needed more copies of a document Jim had told us to bring with us to the crematorium. We told the driver, who drove around the block and then just parked in the middle of the street. He took the papers, jumped out of the car, and disappeared for at least twenty minutes while we sat with the engine running, blocking traffic! Finally, he came back with the copies, and we continued to the crematorium.

Only Bob and I went in. We gave the man in the office the necessary papers and sat there, waiting. I don't remember what we talked about—I think it was Max, Bob's father, who had passed away before I became pregnant with Talia—because I was in a fog. About ten minutes later, the man returned with two small containers, one for me and one for Bob. Inside these brown plastic boxes were our kids. My daughter. Bob's son, Talia's father. It was a surreal moment.

We took the boxes and headed for the airport. I put Talia in my backpack.

At the airport we found my parents and brother sitting off to one side with our luggage. I called Val, the Copa representative, to let her know we had arrived early. All of us had booked different flights for our return because we had had to pick whatever was available in the holiday rush, and she was going to try to get us all out that day. If not for her help, I would have had to fly out the next day, and my parents would have gone back on another airline because all the flights between Christmas and New Year's were full.

Val asked me to meet her at the counter at 3:45 p.m. We had about an hour to spare, so my family and I went upstairs to have some dinner. We just sat there, not really talking. We ate a bit, killing time until our scheduled meeting with the Copa representative.

At 3:45 p.m. we went to the counter, and Val finished booking our flights. I saw Bob and Lynne and Jim W. in line at the other end of the Copa counter, waiting their turn. I felt really bad for them, although, after Bob's selfish behavior, I really shouldn't have. I went over to Bob and told him Copa was taking care of things for us and if they wanted help, he should talk to Val.

He said not to worry about them, they would just check in on their own. So I went back to Val and told her that now it was just the four of us who needed flights, not the other three. I had done my duty; now it was up to him. Val also went over to Bob and introduced herself, and he told her he didn't need any help.

Thirty minutes later, my parents, my brother, and I were all checked in and ready to go. I had no idea what arrangements Bob had made. Val led us straight through security without having to wait in line and up to the Copa first-class lounge. She gave us our own private waiting room and told us she would be back later to take us to the plane. We just stayed in the lounge, resting. We didn't see Bob and the others.

When it was time to head to the plane, Val came for us, and we followed her to the boarding area. She took us to the front of the line, led us onto the plane, and showed us to our seats. Incredible service. I was really impressed with Copa.

Once we had settled in, the plane began to board. Bob, Lynne, and Jim W. got on. Everyone was scattered all over the plane. Bob and I had business-class seats, since we were returning on our original tickets to Panama; everyone else had coach. J. got business class as well because the Copa people accepted Delta miles for his upgrade. They could not have been more helpful.

There I sat, Talia at my feet in my backpack, heading back to the U.S. This was not how it was supposed to be. I was supposed to be sitting next to Talia. I was supposed to be hugging her, not holding onto my backpack with her ashes in it. I was supposed to be going after-Christmas shopping with her, not going home, without her, forever.

CHAPTER SEVEN

CHAPTER SEVEN

DECEMBER 29

The flight to LAX was uneventful. We landed around 10:00 p.m., and once we got through customs, it was quite late. Rather than drive all the way back to Santa Barbara at that hour—and enter my house for the first time without Talia beside me—I decided to stay overnight in an airport hotel. I would make my dreaded entrance in the morning.

My parents, brother, and I left the airport together, and I said goodbye to my dad, who had come down in his own car. My mom and J. decided to stay with me at the hotel so I wouldn't have to be alone.

As soon as we entered the hotel room, I took Talia's computer out of her backpack. I also took out her iPhone, and all her books and papers, and spread everything out on the floor. I wanted the computer and the phone to start drying out; I was really hoping to save them and the information they contained.

Talia loved her phone and her computer, and while I was in Panama she had made a point of telling me, through Rebecca, to be sure to get her computer and her backpack. I was going to do everything possible to save these things. Besides, I needed them. They were part of Talia.

The books and papers were ruined. Her iPhone wouldn't turn on. Her computer screen was smashed in, and there was water behind the glass. Her suitcase was wet and mangled. All of her things had been exposed to moisture for too long.

I wasn't sure how these things had gotten wet. I was under the impression they had remained in the plane until the rescuers found them. They could have been exposed to the rain because the plane had been torn apart. It's also possible the men moved the suitcases and other things out of the plane when they rescued Frankie. Whatever the reason, everything was wet.

After I had spread Talia's things out all over the room, we decided to go to sleep. I felt lost at that moment. I was no longer in Panama on my search and rescue mission, nor was I at home with Talia, sleeping in my own bed. I was in Los Angeles at an airport hotel, and I felt totally useless.

The only reason I had ever had for going home was no longer present. Not in the form I was used to. Yes, Talia was with me, in a little plastic box with a small sticker on it that said *Talia Stella Klein*, and yes, Talia's spirit was with me. But Talia, as I had known her for more than thirteen years, was never going to be there with me again. She would never again be the reason I wanted to get home from wherever I was, whatever I was doing.

The next morning, all I wanted to do was get back to Santa Barbara. J. drove home with me; my mom went back to her house on her own.

I knew my house would be in good order when I walked in. My good friend Georgette had made sure of it. While I was gone, major windstorms had blown the ash from that season's wildfires all over the yard and in through the cracks of every window. Georgette had sent her housekeeper over to clean it up. She knew I wouldn't be capable of cleaning, nor would I want to or even care about it. Never again would I care about something so trivial as dust or folded clothes.

I had asked Georgette to make sure the housekeeper didn't touch Talia's room. I didn't want anyone else making decisions about Talia's things. I didn't want a friend to think she was helping me out by organizing Talia's clothes or removing something from her room. Talia's room was not to be touched. Dusted, vacuumed, OK—tampered with, no. It wasn't that I was going to make Talia's room into a shrine to her, not at all, but I just wasn't prepared to do anything to her room yet.

I hadn't been sure what I was going to feel or how I was going to act when I got home; I didn't know if I was going to break down and cry, or what would happen to me. But when I got home and pulled into the driveway, I felt nothing. And when I went into the house, I felt nothing. It was empty. My house and my life, empty.

I was in a zone. All I knew was that I was no longer the same me that I had been on December 23 at 3:29 p.m., or the same me I'd been the afternoon of December 25. I was no longer Kim, Talia's mom. I was no longer Kim, the barn mom, or Kim, the mom who loved to be with, mentor, teach, and guide her daughter. I was Kim, the mom with the dead daughter. Kim, the mom with no child. Kim, the person who no longer had any idea what to do or say.

I really had to work on getting my memory back. My life with Talia had been slowly coming back to me. I went through all our photos and scrambled to find tangible remembrances of our time together. I gathered the mementos she and I had accumulated on some of our trips, and I started to write down everything I could remember from the moment I got "the Call."

Somehow I was able to exist in that empty house, thanks to friends and family and the entire community, and especially with the help of Talia herself.

It was amazing. Hundreds of people came out of the woodwork to help me in any way they knew how. I was getting deliveries of food, flowers, and plants at least every hour. The phone was ringing off the hook. People were stopping over, one after the other, overlapping. Never in my life would I have thought so many people cared so much about Talia or me.

The most surprising guests of all were Michael's friends and business associates. I received calls, cards, deliveries, and, most of all, personal visits from dozens of Michael's associates, ninety-nine percent of whom I had never met or heard of. Of course, I knew some of them from when we were married or from the community. Michael and I had a lot of friends in common. But it was really touching that so many of his people came to me.

When I say his people, I mean friends and business associates, not family. I received one voicemail from Michael's grandmother, Amy, Talia's great-grandmother, telling me she hoped I could move on. That was it—a voicemail telling me to move on! From someone I thought of as my grandmother. She has never called me again. Ever. On top of that, Michael's aunt, his father's only sister, has never called me or sent me a card. In fact, there is an entire family that has never even acknowledged Talia's death—at least not to me, her mother.

I didn't dwell on this stuff because so much love, generosity, thoughtfulness, and care came from so many other people, but it shocks me so much that I have to write it.

While I was in Panama, I received some of the greatest help from a friend of mine, Jeff, one of Michael's friends from his Young Presidents' Organization group. YPO people stick together like a fraternity, and Jeff was great. He gathered as many potentially helpful International YPO members as possible and had them contact me. The most instrumental to us was Joseph P., the CEO of Copa Airlines. If not for his help and that of Copa, my parents, brother, and I all would have had to fly back on separate flights. That would have been a nightmare, lonely and traumatic. He truly saved the day.

In the midst of all the visitors, and with so many people's help in just existing, I had to look at my life and make sure I was able to survive financially. It was the end of the month, and all my bills were coming due in a couple of days. Normally, I wouldn't have worried about paying them, but because Michael was gone now, I wasn't sure who would be sending me the monthly checks Michael had paid me every month.

The reality of my life was this: I lived solely on the monthly support from Michael. I was a full-time mother, and my only job since Talia's birth had been to be the best mom possible. I was lucky that Michael had been able to pay me enough to enable me to continue being a stay-at-home mom even after our divorce.

You'll recall that back in Panama, when I was lying down in her living room after finding out that Talia and Michael were dead, Linda had come in to tell me that she and her dad had talked about my financial situation and were going to take care of me. At the time, I hadn't known what that really meant, but I figured Bob would just have Michael's accountant send me the checks.

Knowing this had definitely given me some relief from real-world stress for the time being. But once I got home, that relief lasted about two days. I was not prepared for what was about to happen.

I emailed Michael's accountant, Steve, to find out what was going on. I didn't want to have to deal with money yet, but I had

no choice. Steve e-mailed Bob, who then e-mailed me this message: *I understand that when there is no child, there is no obligation to
pay child support. Now that Talia is dead, there is no child, so no child
support. You are going to have to sell your house and get money from
your family.*

I was stunned. How could this be happening? Legally, Bob
was correct—no child, no child support. I knew this, but because
of the circumstances of Talia's death and the fact that Linda had
assured me I would be taken care of, I was under the impression
that my child support checks would keep coming, at least until I
could wind down my financial obligations.

My finances had been based on giving Talia the life she was
entitled to, and this life cost money. I had a house and associated
expenses. I wasn't expecting to be cut off, cold turkey, without
warning or time to plan. My daughter was dead, and I strongly
believed it was because of her father's recklessness. Now not only
did I have to figure out how to live without Talia and how to get
through each moment of each day, but I had no money to pay
my mortgage and other expenses that were due in a few days. I
was getting no help from Bob or anyone else in Michael's family.

I couldn't understand what was wrong with Bob. I was the
mother of his granddaughter; his former daughter-in-law. How
could he be so cold, heartless, and selfish? But there was more.

While we were in Panama, my cell phone was the only one
that worked. Everyone used my phone, Bob included. The lives of
Talia, Michael, and Frankie had depended on my being in constant
communication with anyone who could help us. I didn't even
think twice about using my phone. I didn't care about the cost.

Only a few days after returning from Panama, my cell phone
bill arrived. I opened it, knowing it was going to be huge, and it
was: just under five thousand dollars. If I had been receiving my

monthly checks, this wouldn't have mattered. But I had been cut off, so this phone bill hit me hard.

To top it off, the day after I received the bill, AT&T shut my phone off! Without warning. They said they had tried to contact me to verify that the charges were legitimate and to make sure someone hadn't gotten hold of my phone and run up fraudulent charges—but I had never received a call from them.

Now my phone was disconnected, and they were demanding payment in full before they would turn it back on. I had never once been late, and now, because the bill was high, my phone was shut off. I needed the phone back on. It was still a major communications tool for me, as this was the number most of the world had for me.

I decided to ask Bob if he would pay the cell phone bill. It seemed like a reasonable request. He wouldn't be paying it out of his own pocket, anyway; the money would come directly from Michael's account or through his company. So I asked. "Hi, Bob, I just got my cell bill from Panama, and it's huge. Can you please pay for it?"

He said, "No." *No? Did I hear that right?* He continued, "I'm not going to pay the cell phone bill. I have to pay the $25,000 reward you offered in Panama, so you can pay your cell bill."

I had nothing to say to this. I consciously decided not to argue with him because I didn't want him to tell me that I had to pay the $25,000 reward to the rescuers, since I had offered it against his wishes. It was unbelievable. My daughter was dead—and Bob's son was largely responsible. Yet Bob had cut me off and wouldn't even help me pay a bill he had partly incurred, a bill that was likely the result of his son's actions.

Normally, this sort of blow would upset me, but I didn't cry. In the scheme of my life at the time, this was nothing. It didn't matter what happened to me at this point. No event or circumstance, statement, unkind treatment, or harsh words would ever come close to the enormity of Talia being gone. Yes, I was on the brink of total financial destruction. But my daughter was no longer going to be with me, physically, ever again. Nothing could touch this.

PART TWO
BEFORE PANAMA

CHAPTER EIGHT

MICHAEL'S CHILDHOOD

To this day I don't know why Michael's dad was so cruel to me. Michael and I had always thought of Bob as a kindhearted man. He called himself a Zen Buddhist. How much kinder could a person be than that? But as I look back at how he "raised" Michael and his sister, Linda, I can start to put the pieces together. I can see that Bob was always very selfish and out of touch in his relationships, and his lack of understanding of real love is what made Michael the man he was.

Michael's childhood was definitely not "normal."

His father, Robert G. Klein, M.D., was a highly respected and successful rheumatologist at the Mayo Clinic in Rochester, Minnesota, where the family lived until Michael was two. Then Bob accepted a position at the Sansum Medical Clinic in Santa Barbara, California, and the family moved to Montecito. At Sansum

Bob developed a truly life-changing method of eliminating back and joint pain.

Though Montecito was and still is a very affluent town, Michael did not live the life of the rich and famous. In fact, according to what Michael told me about his childhood, he and his sister lived in conditions that bordered on poverty, and the way they were treated, in my opinion, constituted child abuse.

I must be clear here. I was not around when Michael was growing up. What I am about to say is based on information that Michael told me about his life during the many conversations we had about it, both while we were dating and while we were married.

Michael slept on a mattress thrown on the floor, with a blanket. That's it. Now, you might think his mother *thought* she had a good reason for letting him sleep that way—maybe punishing him for not making his bed or something. But in truth, there was no reason—just lack of care. Michael had no pajamas. His pants were too short, and he was basically a scruffball.

Michael's sister, Linda, was just a baby then. What was her life like? I don't recall what Michael told me about her room or her sleeping situation. I do know that the vines outside the house crawled through the open, unscreened windows and wound up and around the bedrooms, taking over the house and bringing with them bugs, dirt, and little creatures like mice, rats, and raccoons.

The kids' diet was horrendous. Michael told me he and Linda lived on hot dogs. Hot dogs straight from the package, not even warmed up, just cut up and eaten. Now, hot dogs are precooked, but they aren't meant to be eaten cold or to be the staple of a child's diet. Here were a baby girl and a growing boy, living on cold hot dogs. According to Michael, the only other food in the house was cereal and milk.

Michael's Childhood

What were Michael's parents thinking? Michael's mother, Anne, was rarely at home. Though she held a Ph.D. in English, a master's degree, and a couple of other degrees from Stanford, she decided to go back to law school while the children were still young. Her nights were spent in class, her days out studying with friends. Though Bob was a brilliant doctor and researcher, he was unaware that she was absent much of the time. He was at work, and when he wasn't working, he was working out. Running, biking, swimming. He was a health fanatic who was totally oblivious to the rest of life.

When Michael was about eight, his parents divorced and his father moved out of the house. Soon after the divorce, Anne started dating and going away for a day, a night, sometimes even a weekend, leaving the kids *alone*. Michael quickly learned to be independent, but still, you don't leave an eight-year-old and a six-year-old home alone!

Bob had no idea the kids were being left alone, because when he came to pick them up for weekend visits, they would meet him in the driveway. He never asked about Anne.

Forced to care for his sister and himself, Michael's business acumen showed itself early on. From a very young age Michael was fascinated with business. His mentor—really his best friend and the main adult figure in his life—was his grandfather Max, Bob's father. Max Klein was a super-successful businessman who, among other things, was the inventor of Paint By Numbers. He was extremely wealthy, and he knew how to start and run companies and negotiate fantastically well.

Though Max lived in Michigan and Michael in California, they spoke every day from the time Michael was able to talk. Every morning around five o'clock the phone would ring, and it would be Max, calling to speak to Michael. Max would go over what had happened in Michael's life the day before and what he was going to do that day, guiding him with anything that was going on in his life.

He would also tell Michael about his business deals—how he structured them, negotiated them, and got what he wanted. So Michael knew business. It was in his blood. When he was left with the duty of providing for his sister and himself, he knew what to do.

Montecito, which was the home of Julia Child, was a very health-conscious place, and many people were drinking and cooking with goat's milk instead of cow's milk. In fact, a lot of mothers were feeding their babies goat's milk, because it closely resembled human milk. So Michael decided to raise goats and sell their milk to members of the community (including Julia!).

When Michael was about nine, Anne left for the weekend with her boyfriend. By now Michael was accustomed to his mother being gone for a couple of days at a time. But this time, weeks passed, and he figured she was never coming back. She called every so often and made up something about coming back soon, but she never did. Ever.

The only way Michael and Linda were able to survive was through Michael's ingenuity and brilliance. Through his goat's milk business, he was able to make enough money to buy food for himself and his sister. When food ran out, he would get on his bike and ride down to the store to restock. That is how he provided for the two of them for more than a year after his mother left.

By now you're probably thinking that Michael made this up and for some reason I fell for it, but that's not the case. This is unbelievably true. I'm not writing this to hurt Anne; I'm writing it because this is part of what made Michael the man he was.

Of course Michael and Linda couldn't go on living alone forever. Someone was sure to find out. It happened when Michael was about ten.

One day, when Bob came to pick the kids up, he realized he hadn't seen Anne in a really long time and finally asked where she was. Michael broke down and told his dad she had left and never come back. Bob was blown away. Michael said Anne had been gone for more than a year, and he had not wanted to tell because he thought it was his fault she had left. Of course he did! All kids blame themselves when their parents abandon them. So Bob gathered up Michael and Linda and took them home with him.

When Michael told me this story after we started dating, I was aghast. I couldn't imagine a childhood like that. What a dichotomy—growing up with a super-successful father and a mega-wealthy, world-famous grandfather, yet living on the bedroom floor, abandoned by his mother and his totally unaware father. I should have known I was going to have to deal with a very messed-up man, but we were young when we met, and I had no idea what all this was capable of doing to his mind and how it would affect the way he treated people in the future.

For Michael and Linda, living with Bob was not much better than living alone. Bob was still unaware of his children's needs and failed to give them the guidance and supervision they required. But at least they had food.

Bob's girlfriend, Lynne, was worse. She claimed to be an amazing child psychologist, but would call Michael names for eating so much. Instead of helping Michael deal with his mom's abandonment, she only exacerbated the situation. She was so cold to Linda that Linda started acting out against her; one day she cut all the arms off Lynne's cashmere sweaters! Linda wasn't a bad child; she simply had never received any love or guidance, and was doing what any other neglected child would do. Lynne, the psychologist, did nothing to help.

Without supervision, Linda foundered. Michael and I were very grateful that she actually graduated from high school. This was an extremely intelligent girl who could have had all the educational opportunities in the world, and she barely scraped by.

Michael went in the opposite direction. He had skipped so many grades in grammar school that he was taking high-school courses by the time he was in sixth grade. Michael came closest to enjoying a normal school life in middle school. He went to a private junior high where independence was encouraged and students learned to challenge themselves. Michael excelled, and it was there that he formed lasting friendships.

Michael was so advanced that the entire high-school experience was, in his mind, a waste of time. He wanted to move on to the university, earn his degree, and get out in the world and start some companies. Which is exactly what he did.

The University of California at Santa Barbara had a program that allowed high-school students to take college courses for college credit, and Michael signed up. After the first quarter he never went back to high school; he just continued in college. At fifteen years old, he was getting straight A's at UCSB. By the time the school board figured it out, he had so many college credits that they let him skip high school and stay in college.

In college Michael started a couple of companies on his own, founding each company through his own ingenuity and hard work—and advice from his grandfather Max. Never did Michael get a penny from his family.

CHAPTER NINE

THE TIME
BEFORE TALIA

Michael was so far ahead of the game in college that he was taking upper-level courses by the time he was sixteen. I was in two of these classes, which is how we met.

It was my senior year, and, as it turned out, it was Michael's sophomore, junior, and senior year all at once. Both of us had back-to-back classes in the same room, with about a half-hour break between them. One day I was talking to a friend during the break. She and I would talk about all sorts of things, as girls do, and on this day we were talking about our midterm grades. I had received a B+ and was complaining to my friend that I didn't know why.

Suddenly, I had the feeling our conversation was being overheard. I turned around, and sitting behind me was Michael. We hadn't met yet, but I asked him, "Are you listening to us?" He said yes.

I told him if he wanted to get in on the conversation, he was welcome to, so he moved up a row and joined our talk. I told him I was pissed about my grade. He said, "Well, let me see your test." I handed him my blue book, and he perused it. After a couple of minutes he gave it back and said he agreed with the teacher that it was a B+ paper—not enough examples to support my theory. I was surprised—and intrigued. From then on Michael sat with my friend and me and became part of our chat sessions between classes.

This went on all quarter, and by the end of the term, the three of us were really good friends. It was close to the last day of class when somehow birthdays came up, and Michael said it was his birthday. As any new friend would do, I asked him how old he was. He paused, then said, "Seventeen."

I looked at him and, without missing a beat, said, "Wow, that's cool. You obviously skipped some grades." And that was that, at least for the time being. Of course, I was extremely curious, because I knew he must have skipped quite a few grades to be sitting in that class at that age.

On the last day of the quarter, we were talking about what we would be doing over winter break. I said I didn't have much planned; Michael said he was going to Israel with his grandmother. Cool. We all said our goodbyes and headed off. I didn't expect to hear from Michael until January.

Then, out of the blue, I got a call from Israel. Michael was calling just to say hi. He told me about his trip so far. A few days later, I got another call. I started to wonder if there was more to our friendship than I was aware of.

Once Michael returned from Israel, we started going out. Yes, he was five years younger than I, but he was graduating at the same time, having broken the UCSB record for number of units taken per quarter for an entire year. So age didn't make a difference to me.

We finished school, graduated, and began thinking about the rest of our lives. We knew we were going to get married; we just weren't sure when. I changed my plans to go to graduate school in England and stayed in the U.S. to be with Michael. He was planning to work with Max, learning his businesses and starting some new ones. We wanted to start a business together, too.

After years of mentoring, Max had prepared Michael to start, run, and sell basically any kind of business he wanted. Michael was under the impression that he was going to take over all of Max's companies when he graduated.

However, once Michael graduated, his grandfather "changed his mind" and told Michael it would be better for him to stay in California and do his own thing. Michael was angry and unhappy that his grandpa had reneged on his promise. Max, the most important person in Michael's life, had let him down. But, being the creative guy he was, Michael dealt with the blow and moved on.

There was now not a single adult in Michael's life that had not totally betrayed his trust. At the time I had no idea what the ramifications of these breaches of trust would be on the way Michael handled relationships and business for the rest of his life.

After spending the summer learning to scuba dive in Santa Barbara, Michael and I decided it was time to get on with our lives. We moved to Los Angeles, and Michael went to work for a big L.A. real estate developer in order to learn the development business. I wasn't sure what I wanted to do, so I decided to go into the management program at Bullocks Wilshire, a department store that no longer exists. The deal was that I had to start in sales while I waited for the program to start, so I ended up selling clothes for a few months.

While I was at Bullocks, Michael was soaking up knowledge of the real estate world. Always looking for some opportunity, he found a large apartment complex that was in foreclosure in Santa Maria. His boss didn't want anything to do with the project, so Michael went to Santa Maria and met with the owners of the property, an investment group out of Santa Barbara. He came home having struck a deal.

At the time, I was told that the investment group just wanted to dump the property—basically give it to anyone willing to take on the debt and the property itself. (I have since learned that was not true.) Michael ran some numbers and decided to go for it. In January 1989 he bought the apartment complex and moved to Santa Maria to take over the project.

As soon as I could, I moved up there as well, and we ran the complex together. We had to totally renovate the buildings, repair all the units, clean up the place, and rent out the apartments. We decided to manage the property and supervise the work ourselves. Until I actually moved up there, I didn't know that the building was in a really bad neighborhood and had some pretty rough tenants in it. But I didn't care; I could cope with difficult situations.

While we were cleaning up the place, we received death threats from boyfriends of tenants we had had to evict for nonpayment, prostitution, drug dealing, and so on. At times we had quite serious run-ins with tenants in our office. The renovations were done, the place was fully rented, and I was in the middle of planning our wedding when we got the most serious death threat of all.

This threat came from a guy who was in jail. He told us he was getting out in a week and was coming to kill us. He was angry that we had kicked his girlfriend, a prostitute addicted to crack, out of the building. We called the police chief, and he told us this guy was really bad and we had better take the threat seriously. We decided to hire a manager and get out of there. The new manager was a tough guy, capable of handling any situation, and Michael and I moved back to Santa Barbara.

At first we rented the house where Michael had lived with his dad. Bob had bought another house and was planning to rent out the old one, so we became his tenants. Soon after we moved in, Bob decided to sell the house, so we bought it from him. We had to pay market value, but we liked the house, so we did it. We finished planning our wedding there, and that's when I decided to go to law school.

I hadn't always wanted to go to law school. In fact, the thought had never crossed my mind until a friend of mine called and said he was thinking of going to law school in Santa Barbara. I sat there for a moment and thought, *Hey, that sounds like fun; I want to go too.* And that's how I started law school. Ironically, the friend who gave me the idea never went. I was mad at him at first but then decided just to be happy about my decision.

I loved law school. I think I might be the only person on the planet who can say that. I wasn't concerned about passing the bar or practicing—I just wanted the education—so I was more relaxed and could enjoy the experience. Michael and I both knew I wasn't going to practice. I was working with him in real estate, and would later work with him in the high-tech business. Then the plan was that I would be a stay-at-home, full-time mom. So I had no pressure at school, which is probably why I did so well.

During law school we got married, bought a beach house, started a couple of companies, and somehow ended up in a couple of lawsuits. Michael became famous for getting into lawsuits, whether he initiated them or was sued for one reason or another.

It turned out that the apartment complex we had taken over and completely turned around was doing so well that the investment group wanted it back! It was a very complicated situation, but, in short, Michael had taken over the property when it was in foreclosure. He then started to make the payments, trying to take it out of default. But somehow the original owners figured out a way to get the property back, and they did, after a pretty messy fight.

In the meantime, the entire real estate market went down the drain. It was 1989, and even the market in Santa Barbara hit the dirt. So all of Michael's real estate deals needed some tweaking. Michael was the one taking care of business while I was in school, so I didn't know what was happening. In fact, I never really gave it much thought.

Only when I was stuck on the bad end of a fraud suit did I start to wonder what was going on. The woman we had bought our beach house from decided to sue us and try to get the house back. The entire situation got way out of hand, and we ended up going to trial. There I was, close to nine months pregnant, and I had to take the witness stand.

It turned out fine—we won, and no fraud was found. During questioning, all I could say was, "I don't know," because I didn't know. I knew nothing. Michael handled all of our business, and I, the trusting wife, naïve about what he was doing, just signed whatever papers he handed me and went on studying for my law school exams. So when I was asked about the different deals we were in, I had no answers. The judge thought I was an idiot. Looking back, I was pretty much an idiot—not because I was stupid, which I was not and am not, but because I was so trusting of Michael.

We won that suit, and every other suit thereafter. But I'll tell you it was not pleasant having to take the stand and be grilled by the plaintiff's attorney and the judge when I was about to give birth. It was not easy to be accused of fraud and, on top of that, be accused either of being stupid or a Stepford wife.

In the midst of that lawsuit we started a couple of high-tech companies. The first one was a software company that made and sold real estate investment software. While producing that software, we met an amazing programmer named Jim Wolff, and as that relationship evolved, he left Michigan and came to California to live in our home. Then we started another software company called Transoft, which produced device driver software (SCSI). Later, this company invented a new networking system and a way to share data with multiple users, and was later sold to Hewlett Packard.

I was done with law school, had passed the bar, and was working at Transoft. Michael was managing the business end of the company, loving the tech industry, and Jim was handling the programming and other things. Life was good, the future bright.

That's when Michael and I decided to have Talia.

CHAPTER TEN

DECIDING TO HAVE TALIA

Michael and I had been married for five years before we decided to have our first child. I say "first" because the plan was to have four children. It wasn't that we were too busy to have children; we were just young, and neither of us wanted kids that early. There was not even a hint of a "biological clock" ticking inside me until around our fourth anniversary. Up to that point neither one of us had been around any children who helped ignite that spark of desire or wind up that baby clock. But that spark did flare up.

Though Michael and I were born Jewish, we were both agnostic and never went to temple, so we weren't around other Jewish couples and families. We had a real desire to have a culturally Jewish home and to instill in our children a sense of Jewish history, tradition, and values, but we weren't very up on things in that area of life. So, when the opportunity came to learn more about it, we jumped at the chance.

One night we were in Los Angeles at an engagement party for a friend of mine, Jamie, whom I had known since third grade. Jamie had always been a practicing Jew, but after high school she moved to Jerusalem and became more traditional—Hassidic. She also met someone, a rabbi, and they were engaged. It was at their engagement party, at Jamie's mom's house in Los Angeles, that Michael and I met Moshe and Bracha.

Why would two agnostics become friends with a Hassidic couple? What did we have in common? We were all Jewish, and that in itself is always a very strong bond. And Michael and I had a deep desire to learn about our cultural roots and to see a traditional home in action. Who better to learn from than orthodox Jews, who could expose us to the most ancient laws and their meaning.

Bracha and Moshe were extremely generous and warm people. We enjoyed their company, and they enjoyed showing us their way of life, so it was a nice match.

Bracha and Moshe invited Michael and me to numerous Shabbat dinners at their home in Los Angeles. It was then—on our first time at their house, really—that the spark that ignites the desire to have kids hit both Michael and me.

When we first met Bracha and Moshe, they had two children. By the time we stopped going down to Los Angeles for Shabbat, they had four, with a fifth on the way. So they had a great deal of parental experience. They were also very *aware* parents. Both Michael and I saw this in them, and because I knew we would raise our kids with the same kind of awareness, they became role models for us.

We were impressed with Bracha and Moshe's thoughtfulness toward their children. We were even more impressed with the children themselves. These kids were more than just well behaved; they were inquisitive, interactive, highly intelligent, and independent. They were very welcoming to Michael and me. They came up to us and engaged us in conversations that were not "kidspeak" or play-related—actual conversations about real subjects. They wanted to know where we lived and why, and what the people in Santa Barbara were like. They were curious about our business, what we each did in the business, and who are customers were. They literally spoke to us like adults.

There are some amazing kids out there! Michael and I thought. We knew we could have amazing children as well, so we started thinking about having kids of our own.

We were in the middle of major legal hassles, but that didn't interfere with our desire to start a family—the lawsuits were just a blip in our lives. Everything else was going great. Transoft was growing exponentially, and we had to move to larger offices.

Right after the move, Michael decided that he too wanted to go to law school. I asked him if he could handle running the company, waging a big lawsuit, and going to law school, all while expecting a baby. To top it off, we were in the middle of major renovations on the house we had bought, and were trying to get them done so we could move in before Talia was born.

Michael, being Michael, said yes, he could handle it. I knew he could intellectually; I just wasn't sure it was a good idea emotionally or physically. But he wanted to, so I had no problem with it, and he started law school.

The house we were renovating was amazing. It was a huge George Washington Smith design, the first commission of this well-known architect, who was inspired by the Andalusian farm-houses of Spain, and more traditional than his others. The people we bought it from had completely trashed it, so there was a lot of work to do before we could move in.

During the renovations we lived in a trailer in the driveway. I was actually pregnant and in a trailer! My friends laughed, but I really liked living in the trailer. I did want to get into the house before the baby was born, but we knew it was going to be quite a feat.

We made it—by twelve hours! The day finally came when the painters finished and the appliances arrived. I could hardly wait because I needed to cook and have food ready and frozen before I went to the hospital. The minute that stove was delivered, I immediately made a huge batch of spaghetti sauce. Just as I was putting the last container of sauce in the freezer, I felt something. Something strange. It was the beginning of labor. Talk about timing!

I took a shower and went to bed. I knew at some point I would wake up and know it was time, and that's exactly what happened. At 2:00 a.m. I woke up, and off we went to the hospital.

This was December 3, 1994. Michael's birthday. After a really quick delivery without any painkillers, Talia was born. Born on her dad's birthday.

CHAPTER ELEVEN

RAISING TALIA

aising Talia was something I did *consciously*. It wasn't an easy job, though *job* is not the correct word; a truer word would be *honor*. And it was my destiny.

It's not easy to teach, guide, and mentor a child from conception onward. Especially knowing that everything you say or do—and everything that child witnesses, experiences, and thinks about—will have a deep impact on his or her understanding and possibilities in this world and the next. Trying to give Talia information without giving answers, without influencing the direction of her thought or causing walls to be built around her mind, was the most difficult task I could have had. And I loved every moment of it.

At the time I was raising Talia, I didn't know that my influence and guidance would affect her life *after life*. I couldn't have known it then, because that was when I didn't believe in a true afterlife. But I did know that her time on earth, with me in this life, would be molded by my every word and move. And because I wanted not to shape her thoughts and beliefs for her but to allow her to grow and form her own, I had to be extremely diligent.

I watched over myself every second of the day. Each word, action, response—even the inflection of my voice—had to be used precisely to ensure that they were not influencing Talia's thoughts and beliefs but were merely stepping stones for her to walk on while forming her own code for life. Teaching without limiting is the most difficult task there is. My goal was to keep Talia's mind open and not to stifle her or cause the doorways of her mind, leading to all the universe offered, to close.

So, how exactly did I raise Talia? In what way did I raise her differently from the way many people raise their children?

From the moment Michael and I decided to have a baby, I knew I would do whatever I had to do, from preconception throughout the child's life, to ensure our child's maximum health, happiness, and opportunities. I knew instinctively that raising a child starts before you are pregnant. I never really understood why many people don't get this. To me, raising a child is an absolute honor and such a responsibility that not to think about the best way to approach parenthood seems irresponsible to me.

It was time to have a baby. First I made sure I was in the best physical condition possible. I was already playing tennis three days a week, but I started to run a bit as well. It was only three days a week, downhill, and for no more than four miles, but I ran! I was doing something to ensure my circulation was good, my cardio system was functioning properly, and my muscles were toned. I'm not a doctor; I just knew that keeping myself in good physical shape was a good thing.

I also read every book I could find about what to eat before becoming pregnant and during pregnancy to ensure proper nutrition for the baby and me. I knew that at each stage of pregnancy a different organ or system was forming, and each required a special vitamin or mineral. So I simply ate according to what part of the baby was being formed at each stage. I'd eat more of certain vegetables as they were needed, or protein during the weeks it was needed. I made sure I supplied all that was needed to form a healthy baby, and a smart baby too.

Michael and I knew that our baby would be really smart. Michael was beyond brilliant. He was a true genius by IQ, and on top of it he knew how to apply that brilliance in business, which a lot of geniuses don't know how to do. I'm extremely smart myself, and I had smarts in areas where Michael didn't, so together we had a chance to have an amazingly brilliant child.

I also read books about how and what to teach the baby in utero as well as after birth. *Teaching* is not exactly the right word. It was more learning what to say and do to stimulate brain formation and the child's desire to learn more while growing up.

While Talia was growing inside me, both her dad and I would talk to her. We told her stories, I sang the alphabet to her, and, as I went about my day, I described what I was doing. Her dad told her how to make spaghetti. It was quite funny, because as soon as Talia was old enough to have her first taste of spaghetti, she was addicted to it. I'm sure the fact that it's yummy had something to do with it, but talking to her about spaghetti for nearly nine months probably had something to do with it as well!

When it came to giving birth to Talia, I chose to do it naturally. This is a very individual choice people make—and the only choice for me. I had no medications at all during her birth.

Once Talia was born, the real raising began. Basically, I never let her cry. I didn't believe in letting babies cry in order to train them. Not for any length of time anyway. People may say I was overprotective, I spoiled her, I was paranoid, but I saw the fruits of my efforts.

Babies cry for a reason. Whether they're hungry, cold, need to be changed, or don't feel well—whatever it is, they don't cry just because they want attention. A baby is not by nature an insecure attention hound. Babies live according to instinct and cry only for real reasons, so why make them suffer and cry it out? There is no reason, and I believe that so many kids are selfish and insecure, or constantly whine because they were made to cry for extended periods as babies. They had real needs that were not being met, and this affected them subconsciously.

I got a lot of crap from people for responding to Talia as soon as she started to cry. I had argument after argument, but I wasn't going to let someone else dictate how I raised her. In fact, one of the biggest critics of my no-cry theory was Linda, Michael's sister.

One day I decided to let Linda watch Talia for thirty minutes while I ran down the street to get a smoothie. Talia was no more than five months old at the time. I told Linda in no uncertain terms that Talia would be waking up and, when she did, to please give her the bottle of breastmilk I had left for her. I asked Linda to please not let Talia cry, just to pick her up and give it to her—and she agreed.

Well, I was gone for no more than twenty minutes, and I came back to Talia crying in her car seat. Linda was totally ignoring her. I ran in, picked her up, and asked what was going on. Why hadn't she picked Talia up and given her the bottle?

Linda told me she thought it was better to let her cry. I was fuming. I told Linda it was her job to listen to me, Talia's mom, rather than decide what to do on her own, especially after she had agreed to follow my instructions. I also told her she wasn't going to watch Talia again.

By not letting Talia cry for any period of time, I was able to meet all of her needs, her real needs, as a baby. Because I met those needs, there was never a time when she subconsciously thought she was going to starve, remain hot or cold, or be miserable in a wet diaper—in other words, she had no reason to form any insecurities. This was the first step in raising a very secure child.

Another thing I did when Talia was a baby was never to speak to her in baby talk. It's natural for people to walk up to a baby and speak in baby talk because they think it's cute, but what's the purpose? Really, there is none. It's not as if babies are born understanding baby talk and can only learn to speak properly when they're older. A baby is a blank slate, looking to learn from the very beginning, so why not speak to children correctly from infancy and give them the basis to learn languages at a young age?

So, when playing with Talia, changing her, holding her, I always spoke normally. Of course, I put a lot of inflection and animation into my voice, as people do when they speak baby talk, but I was using real words. And I spoke to Talia all the time.

For example, whenever I walked around holding her, I would describe what I was doing. As I picked her up, for example, I'd say, *I'm picking you up, and now we're going to walk into the kitchen, and I'll get out a cup to get a drink.*

Of course, there were times when she might hear me speaking to someone else in a tired or different way. But when I was speaking to Talia, it was always about something real, communicated with presence. I would say, *Now I'm taking off your diaper, now I'm wiping you, now on goes the new diaper.*

The same with getting dressed. As I put the sock on her right foot, I would say, *This is your right sock; I'm putting it on your right foot. In goes your left arm into the left sleeve.* I spoke to her like this about everything. *Let's take a bath. OK, I'm running the water, I'm testing the water, I'm rinsing your hair* . . . and so on.

It seems obvious to me that this is why Talia spoke her first real word, other than "Mama" or "Dada," when she was about six months old. It was an amazing moment.

I was sitting on my bed, holding Talia while I spoke with a good friend who was visiting. I picked up an apple and took a bite. As I bit into the apple, Talia looked at me and said, "Apple." I was blown away, and my friend almost passed out!

That was the start of Talia's speaking career. From that point on she started to repeat words and point and name things. Soon she started to ask for things in full sentences. By the time Talia was a year old, she was speaking in paragraphs—not short sentences but actual paragraphs! Yes, genetics is part of it, but you have to foster a child's natural ability, and by speaking properly to Talia basically from conception on, we definitely fostered her ability to speak.

Even before she could speak, she understood everything I was telling her. I think parents make the biggest mistake in thinking that just because their child cannot say something, he or she doesn't understand what they're hearing. This isn't true at all. Experts say the brain is functioning before children are able to consciously control their tongue movements and make sounds. I've heard that the books you read to children should always be well above their actual reading level, because their ability to comprehend and analyze is well ahead of their speech.

One of our favorite things to do when Talia was a baby was to play kick games and punch games, using hanging toys of different patterns and colors. I got the original idea from a book I read, but I modified it to include all colors, animals, and shapes. I bought a baby toy with little colored animals and shapes hanging from it, and I added some things of my own. I would sit with Talia and show her the dangling toys one at a time, describing them to her. This is the elephant; the elephant is gray. This is the monkey; he is brown. And so on.

Then I would tell her to kick the gray elephant, helping her kick it, and I'd do the same with the other hanging toys. Next I would tell her to kick this or that animal, and she would look at the various toys and kick the right one by herself. We did this until she knew all the animals. Then I would hang a few new animals, leaving up some of the old. And we'd start over.

Soon she knew all the animals and colors. Then I'd hang up a different animal in the same color as another animal and tell her to kick the gray this or that, and she would find it by knowing the color. We played this with her hands as well. It was really fun, and it developed her coordination as well as her mind.

Once Talia was old enough to move from breastfeeding to drinking from a cup, I decided to bypass the traditional sippy cup and go straight to a real cup, a small plastic one. It takes the same coordination for a baby to pick up a real cup or a sippy cup, so why use the sippy? A sippy avoids spills, but it has nothing to do with a child's ability to drink from a real cup.

I didn't just give Talia the cup and let her drink. I helped her a few times by holding the cup with her as she moved it to her mouth to drink. This was really to show her that the cup goes up like this and down to the table again like that. Soon she had that down. I only put water or breast milk in the cup.

I didn't believe in giving her juices at all—too much sugar. Also, I didn't give her cow's milk. I read that cow's milk causes mucus in children and leads to ear infections, and I believe this is correct, though I never tested the theory. I just felt that breast milk from me was what she was supposed to have. Talia never had an ear infection, and she only had mucus when she had a cold.

I didn't give Talia anything other than breast milk until she was five months old. Then we slowly worked in rice, and following that, soup. Though I did buy some baby-food rice to try, it was just too gross looking to give her. I made rice for Talia, whole rice. She started by picking it up with her fingers. She was fascinated with silverware, and as soon as she grabbed for some I gave her baby forks and spoons, and she learned to use them. She stopped using her fingers at a very young age.

Though Talia was very coordinated and really smart, I think all babies can progress as she did if their parents have the patience to teach them. In fact, I feel that kids who use sippy cups and eat with their fingers past a very young age are simply a reflection of lack of training from their parents or caregivers.

I was also very particular about the issue of caregivers. Back then, I lived in a world of housekeepers, nannies, and all sorts of helpers. Most of my friends with kids had nannies. I didn't believe in them. It's one thing if the mother has to work; it's another if she simply wants someone else to help raise her child.

I did have a housekeeper, who lived with us. But I didn't have a nanny. I took care of Talia; the housekeeper, Graciella, took care of the house. There were times when I did let Graciella watch Talia so I could go to the gym or to the market for something quick. But that was when she was close to nine months old, and only for short periods.

I usually took Talia with me to the store. It was another learning experience, plus I loved having her with me. She was what people called a "good baby," so why not take her? I feel she was a good baby because she was being raised correctly. She had no reason to scream for what she wanted or needed. Her needs were all being met.

When Talia began to ask for things, I didn't just give them to her; she had to ask correctly. There was no need to reprimand her in this or any other area. I told her once, "Say please," and she would always say please. Before she began to speak in long sentences, she would say, "More, please," when she wanted more food or drink. As she grew and her language skills blossomed, she would ask in longer sentences: "May I have more spaghetti, please?" Also, if she grabbed for things at the store, I would tell her, "Don't grab, ask." For this reason she was never a kid who ran through the market grabbing everything she was curious about.

It's not that I was strict—I wasn't really. I was to the point. It didn't take much for Talia to understand that certain forms of behavior are acceptable and others are not.

I also differed from my friends on the issue of watching TV. I watched TV, and when Talia was an infant, the TV was on in the background a lot. I did feel that she would learn to speak sooner if she heard people talking. But I didn't use TV as a child amusement center. Never did Talia watch any of the children's shows that other kids watched, nor did I put her in front of the TV to keep her busy so I could do what I wanted. She had toys to play with, she had me to play with. And when she turned two, she had preschool two mornings a week from 9:30 to noon.

Talia loved school from the very first day. She learned to socialize with other kids, share, and eat lunch with others. Gradually she progressed to three mornings a week, and by the time she was five years old, she went four mornings a week. That was plenty. She learned songs and games, played with different kids, learned how to bake bread, and all sorts of things. I didn't leave her there all day; I usually picked her up after lunch to go home with me. On rare occasions I left her until three, and she loved that too.

As Talia grew older she made many friends and had play dates. With play dates came various friend issues. Whose toy this is, who said what, who did what. In time, these issues progressed to dealing with gossip, mean girl issues, who's friends with whom—all totally normal. I feel that the way I helped Talia work through these issues with friends enabled her to become a levelheaded, independent leader who was always true to herself.

The real test of Talia's independence, steadfastness, levelheadedness, and feeling of self-worth started around fifth grade—the age when girls start to mess with each other's heads and learn all the girlish manipulations that cause so many issues throughout junior high, high school, and even adulthood.

Talia had a really great group of friends. She had gone to school with most of them since kindergarten and with some since preschool. Of course, newer friends came into her class in other grades, but she was very close to a core group of kids.

Around fifth grade, many girls started having attitudes—I'm smarter, I'm more popular, that sort of thing. These attitudes emerged in the form of gossip, lying, and being snippy with one another.

Talia never took part in this behavior. She was known as the girl who didn't lie or gossip and who wouldn't put up with this behavior. If she were talking in a group and one girl said something mean about another who wasn't there, Talia would always tell the speaker that it wasn't nice to talk about the missing girl. If the girl didn't stop, Talia would just walk away. She didn't care if she became the subject of gossip when she left the group; she wasn't going to take part in talking behind someone's back.

Talia was very upfront. For example, if she was upset with a girl or felt the girl was upset with her, she would always confront her. Not in an aggressive manner, but nicely. She would call the girl, e-mail her, or tell her in person that she wanted to talk to her. She would then calmly explain that something the girl had said or done had hurt her feelings or upset her in some way. Or Talia would say she felt the girl was mad at her, and she would ask the girl to please let her know if she had done anything to hurt her so they could talk about it.

Talia was known as someone who didn't put up with "bull." Her classmates knew she was the one they could come to for advice and help, the one person they could trust. In fifth or sixth grade Talia was nominated by her peers, and then appointed a special representative whose purpose was to be there for other children to confide in. They would come to her with school issues or personal problems, and she would help guide them, always confidentially. It was quite an honor to be trusted so much by her friends and teachers.

I always knew that Talia was instrumental in keeping her circle of friends together, but it wasn't until after the accident that her friends and their parents told me just how instrumental she was. It seems Talia was always there to bring the class together. For example, at dances, when boys and girls would hang out on opposite sides of the dance floor, Talia would grab people and bring them all into the center to dance. Or if one friend had an issue with another, Talia would help mediate their interaction until they came to a peaceful resolution.

Many of the parents who were my friends told me that after the crash, without Talia at school, the whole social structure broke down. There was a huge hole that could not be filled, and the equilibrium of the upper school was put off balance. Many of Talia's friends were lost and had no one to turn to. I always knew Talia was at the core of her group, but hearing how integral she was and what a positive influence she had had on her friends and her school made me smile and laugh, and at the same time feel so sad for her friends.

It's not that Talia could handle anything and everything or that she was without conflict. She was human. It was the way she handled the issues that arose, and her good sense in coming to me when she didn't know how to handle them, that really made her stand out.

Often, things would occur that Talia didn't know how to handle. When this happened, she would always come to me for advice. This is where the real teaching took place. I had to think deeply before uttering a word when Talia asked me how she should handle a situation; it takes great concentration and forethought to give the right advice to a preteen girl. It's easy for girls to be mean to each other, and honestly, mothers are just older girls. Moms often say the wrong thing to their daughters, thereby perpetuating the mean-girl issues.

For example, when a daughter tells her mom that another girl in school wears too much makeup or dresses inappropriately, the mother might comment to her daughter, "Well, of course she does, look at how her mom dresses." Instead of pointing fingers, it would be better for the mother to ask her daughter why she thinks the other girl is dressing this way and whether there's any way she can help her friend become more aware of her appearance.

It's difficult to give real-life examples of what I did without breaching Talia's confidence or that of her friends. The fact that Talia isn't here in the body doesn't give me the right to spill her secrets or expose her friends to embarrassment. But I will try to illustrate what I'm talking about with some real-life events.

Once, while on a class camping trip, Talia was partnered up with a girl in her class and shared a tent with her. This girl was a good friend of Talia's but not her best friend. The teachers wanted to foster new relationships by splitting up known groups and having the kids work and hang out with other kids.

Talia's partner was very sweet and polite but could also be gossipy, as most girls are. She was a bit jealous of Talia and Frankie because they were so close. One night in the tent, before falling asleep, this girl started to tell Talia all of Frankie's "secrets." She actually made up these stories in an attempt to put a wedge between Talia and Frankie. She felt that if she could make Talia believe Frankie was sharing her secrets with someone else and not with Talia, Frankie and Talia would split up. The girl was also jealous of Frankie and wanted to hurt her by telling Talia outright lies about Frankie's family.

What Talia did was perfect. Instead of falling for the ploy and getting upset, Talia confronted the girl as soon as she had finished telling all these lies. She told the girl that not only would Frankie not tell her any of this, it was unacceptable for her to be making up lies, especially such hurtful lies. Talia said she wasn't going to put up with it and told the girl she needed to apologize to Frankie the next morning. The girl didn't do this; instead, she decided to perpetuate the lies. She told other girls at the camp that both she and Talia had been talking about Frankie, and then made up things Talia had supposedly said to her! Talia was very upset, and rightfully so. As soon as she returned home, she told me everything and asked me what to do.

Now, this was a very complicated situation. Talia didn't want to tell on the gossipy girl, yet she didn't want to be spoken of as part of the hurtful gossip that was being spread. Finally, she didn't want her best friend to be hurt when she found out what was being said. I had to be really careful how I advised Talia to handle this. I gave her options and told her to think them through and see which one she felt best with.

As a first option, I told her she could go to her adviser, describe the conversation in the tent, and ask for advice. This would do two things. It would let the adviser know that Talia wasn't the instigator of the hurtful gossip, nor did she help to perpetuate it. Also, the adviser might already be aware of this gossipy girl's behavior and have a good idea how to handle this situation.

The second option I gave Talia was to go to Frankie and explain what happened in the tent, tell her what the other girl said, and let Frankie confront the gossiper herself. Finally, Talia could opt to do nothing and let the chips fall where they may, recognizing that the first story out there is the one people are likely to remember and accept as "the truth."

Talia thought about it and decided to go to her adviser for advice. The adviser went with her to tell Frankie, and everything worked out fine. Talia and Frankie's relationship stayed strong, and the gossipy girl was reprimanded for her lies. This wasn't the first time she had lied, and the school was grateful Talia reported the incident.

Talia really showed her ability to think independently and remain true to herself when she attended a horse show in Tucson with her dad, his girlfriend Bronwyn, and Bronwyn's children Sean and Charlotte. Talia was sitting at the table with her dad, Bronwyn, and Sean when Bronwyn started to tell Michael the length of Sean's legs. Talia asked why he needed those measurements. No one said anything. Talia repeated, "Why do you need these measurements?" Again, silence. Michael, Bronwyn and Sean all acted as if she were not even there.

Talia was angry and hurt. After being ignored twice, she said, "Dad, what's going on?" Bronwyn then said, "Your dad needs Sean's measurements because he's going to buy Sean a new pair of jeans," or something to that effect. Talia later told me that when she heard this she was really hurt, not because of the jeans, but because they had all totally ignored her for no reason. As soon as it was time for her to show, Talia got up from the table and walked away.

When Talia was alone with her dad, she told him that it was not only rude of him to ignore her and treat her as if she didn't exist, but that his buying jeans for Sean was a really stupid reason to have been so mean to her. Her dad told her he wasn't buying Sean jeans at all; he had no idea why Bronwyn had said that. She was giving him Sean's leg measurements so he could help Sean find the right size bicycle.

That really made Talia mad. On top of being ignored, she had been lied to for no reason. Apparently, Bronwyn was trying to hurt her. Doing what I had always told her to do, Talia let her father know exactly how she felt about the whole incident. Michael apologized, and that in itself was very significant for Talia. I had always taught her not to ignore her feelings, to face them and get them out. It wasn't easy for her to do this with her father, but she did, and I was very proud of her.

There was a lesson in this, and Talia quickly grasped it. When she came home and told me about the incident, she asked me why I thought her dad and Bronwyn had been so mean to her, and why Bronwyn felt she had to lie to her in the first place. Now, it would have been very easy for me to badmouth Bronwyn and Michael, but I didn't. I simply told Talia the truth: I had no idea why either of them would do that, but I was very proud of her for letting her father know that he had hurt her and that she wasn't going to accept such treatment from him or anyone else.

That was the real lesson, anyway. Talia was learning to acknowledge how she felt and to let others know when they had hurt her. Not many adults are in touch with their feelings, and even fewer are strong enough to confront someone in order to have their feelings acknowledged and understood.

In raising Talia, I tried to lead by example. Since we were together so much, Talia was often with my friends and me when we talked on the phone or visited. She would hear how I handled a particular situation, and after I hung up the phone, or when we were alone together, she would ask me why I had said this or done that. I would always explain my reasoning.

Talia amazed me with her insight about one of my friends, and this time it was she who gave me a talk. This friend is a very big gossip, but she has a wonderful, giving heart. I've learned over the years that, in order to preserve our friendship, I must not tell her anything that I don't want to get out. I had to learn this lesson the hard way.

You may think she's not a true friend if this is the case, but she doesn't gossip out of ill will; she truly thinks she's helping you when she tells your secrets. When you need help, she wants to rally the troops, so to speak, even if you tell her not to.

One day, when I told Talia we were going over to this friend's house for dinner, she said she didn't want to go, and didn't understand why I wanted to go, either. I asked Talia why she felt this way, and she told me she thought this friend was a gossip, and talking about other people behind their back wasn't nice. She said if this friend tries to talk about other people to me when they're not there, surely she talks about me to other people when I'm not there. Why would I be friends with someone like that, she asked.

Wow, Talia was right. I explained to her that sometimes the positive does outweigh the negative, and in this particular relationship certain things were important to me. I told Talia that although I was fully aware of my friend's behavior, I was able to shut off her gossip as it occurred and keep our friendship at the same time. But it really impressed me that Talia was so aware of this woman's behavior that she made a point of letting me know I needed to be aware as well. She knew the difference between a positive and negative conversation and was strong enough not to be caught up in the negative when people came to her with gossip. Yet another lesson many adults still have not learned!

By the time Talia was 13, I had guided and mentored her on so many occasions that she was really adept at reading situations and handling them herself. I wasn't needed as a preemptive adviser so much and became more of a sounding board when Talia wanted to talk about the way she had handled a sensitive issue.

It's important to realize that by the time a child is a preteen, his or her views on truth, justice, what is right and what is wrong are already formed. From the moment they're born, children's views are influenced by every word you speak to them and every example you give in the way you live your life in front of them. I don't believe in a "Do as I say, not as I do" way of life. I don't think that teaches children anything, and that's not how I raised Talia.

I'm very proud of how Talia turned out, and I have no regrets about how I lived my life in front of her or with her. I have no regrets about how I helped her handle every situation that arose. Talia lived her life graciously, gratefully, generously, and honestly, and I will always be thankful for having her in my life, and for the love we shared and still share.

CHAPTER TWELVE

DIVORCE

I t wasn't always easy to give good, sound, non-emotional advice to Talia as she was growing up. It was especially difficult because I was the only parent actually there to give her the advice and guidance she needed.

When Talia was around nine months old, Michael decided to add business school to his schedule. While running our company and attending law school at night, he enrolled in the MBA program at Pepperdine University's School of Business.

You may think he was crazy for taking on so much study while running a company, but Michael was very talented, and he had a photographic memory. It really wasn't an intellectual challenge for him. It did, however, become a personal challenge for me.

Michael was in Pepperdine's Executive MBA program. That meant he went away to class on the weekends rather than on a daily basis, either to the satellite campus in Westlake Village or fellow classmates' businesses around southern California. The first weekend of his MBA program was a get-to-know-you weekend. This is where the problems started.

From the moment Michael returned home after that first weekend, he was no longer the husband and father he had been when he left. It turned out that a woman in Michael's program had decided to go after him.

This woman, Robin, was much older than Michael and me, and she had been married before. She was in Michael's core group at school, and I later heard that as soon as Michael had given his life history and described his goals and his company, she began to pursue him.

When Michael came home from that first weekend away, he asked me if I cared if he was friends with "a girl." "Of course I don't care," I told him, "you can be friends with anyone you want." But the fact that he asked me was a signal that there was more to it. I asked him about Robin, and he told me that not only was she gay, but he wasn't attracted to her at all—another red flag. I had really great instincts, and I knew something was up. But I didn't say anything. I just let it be.

Well, the next weekend Michael decided to take my BMW instead of his truck to class. Now that was strange. Why would he care about what car he was driving? I wasn't happy, because I was home with Talia and needed a big, safe car to drive her around in, but he took my car and left me with his little Nissan truck. It turned out Michael wanted to show off his success by taking the 750iL.

Michael started coming home later after his weekend classes. Then, one weekend he put his mountain bike in the back of his truck and stayed away an extra day, telling me he was taking a day off to go mountain biking with his new lesbian friend.

Divorce

Soon he stopped telling me what hotel he was staying at. This was back when cell phones were just emerging, and we didn't have them yet, so, not knowing where Michael was staying, I had no way to reach him in an emergency. And with a baby, a business, and a big house, there was always something to deal with.

It was after his second MBA weekend that Michael came home and told me he was hiring Robin to be the new vice president of marketing for our company. He said he had to hire her because we were starting to organize the company to take it public soon, and he needed more officers.

I told him this wasn't a good idea. He didn't really know Robin, and she had *no* experience or knowledge of the high-tech world; she was currently working for a hair-care manufacturer. I also told him it wasn't right to hire someone he had just met at school, and what was more, I wasn't comfortable with the whole idea; I thought she had ulterior motives, and I hadn't even met her.

Michael, in his typical Michael way, told me he didn't care what I thought; she was hired. With no warning he told me she was coming over, and the three of us, along with Jim Wolff, another director, and his wife, were all going to dinner. He arrived home, and Robin followed. In they walked. I can't say how I knew, but I just knew: she had a plan, and it was to get Michael, his company, and his money.

I soon found out that Jim Wolff didn't want Michael to hire Robin either. But Michael, being a controlling person, didn't care. He was up to something. What put the cherry on the sundae of obviousness to me was that in her employment contract Robin insisted she be allowed to fly first class on any business trips. Michael agreed. Now, Michael didn't even fly first class. He thought it was a waste of money.

Robin started to work at the company around October, a month after Michael had met her. At that point Michael started to stay away from home for a couple of days beyond the business school weekend, and he told me I couldn't come to the office any more. That was totally unacceptable. I was co-owner of the company, an officer and a director.

Jim was also a part owner as well as a director, and he was really unhappy with the way things were being run. He approached Michael and told him he didn't like Robin and didn't like the way Michael was running things any more, and Michael basically told him to stuff it. Jim had no choice but to put up with the situation.

By Christmas, three months after the start of Michael's MBA program, life was totally different. He was never home to see or play with Talia, he was missing in action for most of the week, and he was basically telling me and everyone else to stuff it, saying it was his life. It was clear as day what was going to happen next.

Michael didn't come home after his law school finals in December. Instead, the morning after his last final, a couple of days before Christmas, he called me from LAX. "I'm taking a little break for a bit, back in a few days." That's what he told me! He probably wouldn't even have told me this much except it was Christmas time, and to just disappear over the holidays would have been unconscionable.

I had found his plane tickets and his bags in the truck the day before, so I already knew he was at LAX. When I found the tickets, I took a good look at them, and there was a ticket for Robin as well. They were going to Hawaii together. And Michael had paid for it on our charge card. Unbelievable! So when he said he needed a little getaway, I told him I knew he was at LAX, and I knew he was going to Hawaii with Robin. I told him he was an ass and hung up.

Divorce

You might ask why I didn't file for divorce while he was gone. There were a couple of reasons. First of all, I had a little baby. I didn't want her to grow up in a divorced home. Also, I really thought Michael was going through something, and we would work through it, and it would be over. He was only eighteen when we married, and he had been working really hard ever since. I thought he was freaking out a bit with a new baby too. A little freak-out was normal, and things would be OK soon. Well, I was in denial, and I was totally wrong.

When Michael got home from Hawaii, he didn't come home to see his baby or me. He went to Robin's.

That New Year's Eve, Santa Barbara had the most powerful windstorm in history. Power poles had fallen across the freeway; there were power outages everywhere. I got home that evening to find my huge electric gate had been pushed backwards. The winds were so strong that I had to use my car to push it open. Also, some large oak trees had fallen, branches had gone through some windows, and the power was out. Michael didn't even call to find out how his baby was.

I took Talia to the Biltmore Hotel, where we stayed for a few days. As soon as the power came back on, we were able to go home. I had the windows fixed and cleaned up the mess. No Michael. I was pissed. I called Robin's house. Michael didn't know I knew he was there; he thought he was being sneaky. But I wasn't stupid. When Robin answered, I just asked for Michael. She didn't know what to do, so she put him on. All I told him was that he was a total jerk for not even caring about his baby in this windstorm, and hung up.

A few days later, when I came home from tennis, I walked into our room and found all the French doors open. The curtains were flying in the wind. I looked in the closet. Michael had taken most of his clothes. He had sneaked out the bedroom doors so the housekeeper wouldn't see him. He was too much of a wimp to tell me to my face that he was leaving and take his stuff out the front door in a suitcase.

I tried to call Michael and talk to him, but he wouldn't talk to me. He was being an immature, selfish idiot. It wasn't that his wanting to leave was wrong, it was how he did it. He wouldn't tell me he wasn't happy, he wouldn't tell me he needed space; he just left. I knew it had been coming, but to be so sneaky? Stand up, be a man, and tell me. Don't sneak away—be upfront about it.

But the story gets a lot worse. Right before Michael left, he stopped depositing his paychecks into our account. I had to pay the household bills, go to the grocery store, and take care of Talia, and he claimed the company wasn't paying him because it was having money issues. I knew that wasn't true. The company was about to go public; there was no way he wasn't getting paid. I went to the office, looked in his drawer, and found a checkbook for a new account. He was depositing his pay into that account.

From that moment on, it was a struggle to get anything from Michael. That was true during the divorce and for the rest of his life.

Michael filed for divorce, and I was served with papers that included a restraining order to keep me out of the company. Michael had totally perjured himself in the documents. He claimed I was threatening Robin, which was interfering with business. He also said I was a martial arts expert and a gun expert.

None of this was true. I had never threatened Robin, nor was I interfering in the business. I was home basically twenty-four hours a day taking care of Talia. I had studied aikido in the past but was in no way an expert, and besides, my style of aikido was passive. I did shoot at the time, and both Michael and I had guns, but I wasn't an expert then (some would consider me one now).

Michael knew these things would strike emotional chords. He had thrown in that stuff about my being a martial arts and gun expert to get the judge riled up and to try to keep me away from the company.

At our first hearing, the judge dismissed the restraining order and, in fact, ordered Michael to allow me inside *my* company whenever I wanted to go. He also ordered Michael to give me access to all company records and to permit me to come in and make copies during normal business hours. Michael tried to get the judge to order me to stay away except to make copies after hours, but the judge saw through him completely.

Without going into detail about our divorce proceedings, I will say that Michael was ordered month after month to pay me support—but he didn't. In fact, he filed a motion with the court to have me pay him! That sent the judge over the edge. He told Michael he had twenty-four hours to pay me all arrearages and current support or he would be thrown in jail.

That did it. Michael finally paid me. But for six months I had gone without money from him. I had a baby, Michael's baby, to take care of; I was a full-time mom; and he wanted me to pay him! I was able to take care of Talia with money I got from my mom, but if it hadn't been for her, I wouldn't have been able to buy food. No exaggeration. The court documents speak for themselves.

During the divorce I was forced to move out of the house. Michael wasn't giving me any money, and I was told that whoever lived in the house would have to pay the other person rent. It was a huge house that required a lot of maintenance, and I couldn't afford that.

So here I was, single, with a baby. A baby whose father never saw her and who tried to abandon his responsibility to take care of her and me. Not what I had imagined for her life or mine.

CHAPTER THIRTEEN

DEALING WITH MICHAEL

Dealing with Michael after the divorce was never pleasant—it ranged from neutral to unpleasant. He was cold and distant, and he made no effort to be nice to me. He didn't even apologize for the way he had left or for his subsequent actions.

For the first year after the divorce, Michael rarely saw Talia. It turns out he wasn't a baby guy. I never stopped him from seeing her. In fact, I would frequently invite him to come over and play with her. I told him he was welcome to hang out and interact with her at my house or in the yard, visit her, feed her, even take her with him for visits. But he didn't do any of this.

After our separation and before the divorce was final, a period of about 18 months, he probably saw her no more than ten times. A few times he did pick her up and take her to his house, the house I was forced to move out of, to visit with his mom and her husband, but these rare visits lasted only a few hours.

Talia nursed until she was twenty-two months old, but this didn't in any way prevent Michael from spending time with her. By the time Talia was a year old, nursing was a comfort and bonding thing for her, not a requirement. So the fact that Michael spent little time with Talia was entirely of his own doing. We had a visitation schedule in place that stated he would take Talia on Tuesday nights and every other weekend. I think he started to do this just after her second birthday.

I was always happy when Talia went with Michael. She needed to spend time with her dad. I wanted them to be close. We had gotten a divorce, but that didn't mean Talia had to feel the effects of it. Too many children from divorced homes have terrible relationships with one or both parents. They're insecure, they manipulate their parents to get what they want, and they grow up feeling at fault that their parents are not together.

I didn't want this for Talia. I know Michael didn't want that for her either, though we never talked about it. Michael wouldn't talk to me about anything. He was basically silent when he came to get Talia and when he brought her home. It was very uncomfortable, and I tried not to let Talia see or feel how hard it was for me. I don't think she knew how bad dealing with her father was until she was a lot older and had to deal with him herself.

There were times when Talia didn't want to go with her dad. A couple of times when he came to get her, she clung to me, screaming and crying that she didn't want to go. That broke my heart, and it killed me to have to make her. On both occasions I tried to calm her down by talking to her, explaining that she would have fun, telling her to go and have a nice time, and that I'd be there when she got home. She clung harder to me, and Michael had to grab her and pull her away. He seemed to be unaware that his actions were hurting Talia, and that he was handling the situation all wrong. I tried to talk to him about it on the phone afterward, but he wouldn't listen.

One day his mom, Anne, came with him to get Talia, and again Talia screamed and clung to me. Anne did nothing to help. She allowed Michael to grab Talia, and they both literally ran down the steps and jumped in the car. Talia wasn't even in her car seat when they sped off. I was totally unnerved. I thought, *If they're that unsafe with Talia in front of me, what goes on that I cannot see!* Also, I had expected Michael's mom to become a bit more maternal with age, but obviously she hadn't.

Eventually, he started taking Talia every other weekend from Friday night through Sunday morning. You have to understand, I was totally up for Michael having Talia as much as he wanted. I really wanted them to be close. I also liked having a bit of free time. Since I was a full-time mom, I was always with Talia. Though I loved every minute we were together, I did want some time to myself.

For awhile he was pretty reliable about picking her up for dinner Friday night, keeping her overnight, and bringing her home on time. But Michael's life was his life, and nothing was going to interfere with it. If he wanted Talia one weekend, he took her; if he didn't, he would cancel, sometimes without notice. I pretty much went along with whatever he wanted in order to keep the peace and because I did want Talia to see him. I never understood those mothers who don't allow the fathers to see the kids. It feels unhealthy to me, counter to the best needs of the child. Talia's needs mattered most to me. Always and forever.

Even at this young age, Talia would come home from her dad's and tell me about her weekend. Sometimes she had fun, sometimes she didn't. Occasionally she would be upset about something Michael had said to her. When she was about four years old, she came home and told me she never wanted to go back to Daddy's again.

I asked her why. Her answer was, "I hate Robin." I wasn't going to dig into this one. Contrary to what Michael liked to tell people, I never badmouthed Robin to Talia, nor did I badmouth Michael to Talia. So when Talia told me she hated Robin, I was very factual and unemotional. "Why do you hate her?" I asked.

Talia proceeded to tell me that she was in the kitchen with Robin and asked if she could help her cook, and Robin turned around and yelled, "Go to your room!" Talia had done nothing wrong—she was just asking to help out. She loved to stir, add ingredients, and try to cut up vegetables. But Robin apparently was in a bad mood and took out her anger on Talia. With this, Robin started down a road of cruel and cold behavior that would last as long as she was with Michael.

A few times Talia came home and told me she had had an OK weekend. She would tell me that while she was out shopping with her daddy and Robin, Robin had picked out a top or a sweater and bought it for her, which Talia thought was nice. But the times of generosity and niceness toward Talia were few and far between. Talia didn't care about gifts, anyway; all she wanted was for Robin to talk to her and listen to her, not to ignore and mistreat her.

When Talia was old enough to get on a horse, about five, she asked me for riding lessons—partly because she knew I used to ride a bit when I was young, partly because she herself liked horses. And when she went to the barn with Robin and her dad, she had seen Robin ride.

I found a trainer and enrolled her in lessons at a barn near home. Later, she also took lessons at the barn where Robin rode.

As time went on, it became apparent that Talia loved to ride, was great at it, and needed to be at one barn only. So, giving in to Michael, who thought Talia should ride at Robin's barn, I stopped taking Talia to the barn I had found for her, and she started riding full time at the barn where Robin rode.

That's when a lot of problems flared up. When Talia had improved to the point that she was ready to start showing, Robin refused to allow her to show at any show for which she, Robin, was scheduled. Since Robin rode in every one of the trainer's shows, that meant Talia couldn't show.

This became a huge issue for Talia and for me. After all her hard work, Talia wanted and deserved to show. To compound the problem, Robin finally allowed Talia to show but insisted that I not be there. This really hurt Talia. Robin had always put herself first, and now she was hurting Talia by telling her that her mom couldn't come watch her show. This was cruel and totally unacceptable to me. Robin's selfishness became the basis of many arguments between Michael and me and was the subject of prolonged negotiations in court related to support modification.

When I attended Talia's first real horse show in Orange County, Robin made a scene. I had watched Talia ride her first class in the morning and was waiting for her to ride again when Robin started yelling and cussing at the trainer's assistant, saying she wouldn't show if I was around. She did this in front of Talia! All the spectators heard her. It was so awful that I left the area and didn't see Talia show for the rest of the day. Talia was really upset that I didn't see her win her first A-level blue ribbon. This was the show that triggered a costly legal battle.

Robin's behavior around the barn and at shows is just one example of how she treated Talia. Often, when Talia came over for the weekend, Robin would either leave to show or go to the spa with her friends. It wasn't that she wanted to give Michael time alone with Talia; she simply wanted nothing to do with Talia. Sometimes Robin would stay home when Talia was there and ignore her the entire weekend. No wonder Talia hated Robin. I wasn't pleased, of course, that Robin made my daughter feel so bad, but there wasn't anything I could do except help Talia work through her feelings once she got back home with me.

The situation with Robin never got better for Talia. Once, Talia was at a horse show with Robin and her dad, and Robin actually told Talia that she "sucked," that she wasn't good enough for this particular horse. Some people would say Talia was exaggerating when she told me things because that's what kids do. But that wasn't the case. Talia didn't lie, exaggerate, say things to get attention, or tell you what she thought you wanted to hear. Talia was the most honest and rational kid—person, really—there was. If she said something happened, it happened, and it happened the way she said.

Most of the time people witnessed Robin's cruelty to Talia. Robin had no control and would often lash out and say mean things in front of the trainer, other clients at the barn, and whoever else was within earshot. Her reputation in the riding world wasn't good, and her reputation as a stepmother was just as bad. Robin wouldn't even allow her phone number to be on Talia's school emergency list.

Once Michael figured out that Robin was not who he thought she was, he left her. But he didn't leave her nicely; he didn't learn from his mistakes with me. He cheated on her, left her, went back to her, then left her again. All that time Talia knew what was going on!

Talia would come home and tell me that over the weekend she and her dad had hung out with some other woman and her kids.

She asked me if I thought Daddy was cheating on Robin. I said I had no idea. But the fact that my eleven-year-old daughter knew what cheating was, and was being put in the middle of her dad's relationship with his wife and his new girlfriend, was wrong!

I told Michael that Talia had asked if he was having an affair, and he just laughed. I tried to tell him he had to be cognizant of his behavior around Talia; she was learning from our actions. He just told me to butt out. So I had a really hard job trying to teach Talia without slamming her father, who was supposed to be a role model.

At the same time I couldn't condone his behavior. Striking this balance was one of the hardest things I've ever done. And Michael didn't do a thing to help me. He kept taking Talia to hang out with his girlfriend. During one of his breakups with Robin, he even had Talia sleep at his girlfriend's house with him! That blew me away. I let him know that this was totally unacceptable. He proceeded to tell me that he and I had two different styles of parenting. Yes, we did!

The last couple of years of Talia's life with her dad were basically miserable. He went from having a totally selfish and cold wife, who treated Talia heartlessly, to teaching Talia that it is OK to cheat on your wife, sleep at your girlfriend's house, and date a few other women simultaneously while lying to your girlfriend.

At first, Talia and I were both really happy about Michael's prospective relationship with his new girlfriend, Bronwyn. Starting out, life with her was better for Talia than it had been with Robin. Though I was displeased that Talia knew about Michael's relationship issues, the fact is, she did, and I helped her deal with them.

When Talia first got to know Bronwyn and her kids, Michael was still married to Robin. Talia actually enjoyed the new group dynamics. Though she never had any alone time with her dad, it was better than being around someone cold and disinterested. Bronwyn was warm, fun, and very interested in Talia's life—at least for the time being.

When Bronwyn set her sights on Michael, she was still married and living in Northern California. Once she met Michael, she decided to leave her husband and move the kids to Santa Barbara. Without warning, she tried to get up and go. Her soon-to-be ex was caught by surprise.

The night before Bronwyn's moving truck was to pick up her things, she told her husband she was leaving him and taking their daughter with her! He was floored that she was trying to take his daughter away from him without any notice. (Bronwyn's son has a different father.) He immediately filed a motion in court to keep the girl with him and was able to arrange a week-on, week-off schedule to see his daughter, but Bronwyn still took her. Without notice, she moved away with the kids and immediately enrolled her son, a year older than Talia, at Talia's school.

My formal introduction to Bronwyn was in the parking lot of Talia's school on the first day after the holiday break in 2006. While dropping off the kids in the morning, Bronwyn saw Talia. She saw that I was her mom and came over and introduced herself to me. My first impression was pleasant. She was nice, and she seemed truly interested in getting to know Talia and me better. Bronwyn called me up later and invited Talia and me to lunch so we could all get to know each other.

Bronwyn and I hit it off and became friends. It was great because I really thought that if Michael did in fact leave Robin and stay with Bronwyn, things would be better for Talia, and my relationship with Michael might ease up. There would be no more Robin to control Talia's riding and showing. Over the next few months Bronwyn, the kids, and I spent a great deal of time together.

To my dismay, however, Bronwyn was extremely open with her kids about her love life. It turned out that she was very vocal in front of Talia about her affair with Michael and wanting to have kids with him. We would all be having lunch or breakfast at the café we frequented, and she would talk about her and Michael's plans. I told Michael of my displeasure with Bronwyn's openness about their relationship in front of the kids. He agreed that it wasn't appropriate for Talia to hear all this from Bronwyn, but he didn't do anything about it.

While Michael wavered between Robin and Bronwyn, Bronwyn and I remained close. It wasn't uncommon for her to call me, upset about Michael.

At the end of 2006, Michael was in the middle of a huge lawsuit with the former employees of his hedge fund. During the trial he put his relationship with Bronwyn on hold because he needed to focus on the trial. He also wanted to keep Robin on his side because she was working very hard, helping him with the trial. He was basically keeping her around for that reason. He planned to dump her after the trial was over and then go public with his relationship with Bronwyn. I don't think Robin was aware of this.

Right after the trial was over, when Bronwyn expected Michael to give Robin the boot for good, Michael told Bronwyn he was breaking up with *her* and staying with Robin. He then told Bronwyn he was taking Robin to Panama the next weekend instead of her. Bronwyn had been looking forward to that trip with him, and she was crushed.

She was also very angry. She wanted to get back at Michael and asked me if I would go to Panama with her to spy on Michael and Robin. "No way," I told her. "I'm not doing that; I want no part of it." Then she asked if we would go to Hawaii with her to get away. That I would do. So Talia and I went with Bronwyn and her son on a long weekend vacation to Hawaii.

Michael's relationship with Bronwyn continued to be on-again, off-again. When we returned from Hawaii, Michael told Bronwyn he had changed his mind once more and was in fact going to divorce Robin. He just had to wait a little while so she wouldn't think he had used her to help him through the trial. So Bronwyn and Michael got back together.

But even though Michael had filed for divorce, Bronwyn found out that he wasn't planning on marrying her, as she had thought. It seems that while Michael was dating Bronwyn, he had joined Match.com and was meeting many other women. Bronwyn found his advertisement and was pissed. Besides not being honest with Bronwyn, Michael told Talia all about his intermittent relationship with Bronwyn and the many women he was meeting through Match.com.

Sometimes Talia would come home and tell me all about her weekend with Bronwyn and her kids. Other times she would tell me that Daddy had left her home alone Saturday night while he went on a date with a woman from Match.com. I let Michael know that he should keep his personal life separate from his life with Talia until he was involved in a serious relationship. He told me to butt out. So, when Talia came home crying and mad at her dad, I had to deal with it.

CHAPTER FOURTEEN

TALIA'S LIFE WITH HER SINGLE DAD

One of the worst times for Talia began when Michael did in fact leave Robin for good. He started dating Bronwyn openly, and Bronwyn thought she had won the prize. She really thought she and Michael were going to get married, and her confidence in their relationship was at an all-time high. So much so that her real motives and personality began to show through.

Once Bronwyn thought she had Michael, she blew me off. She did this after we got back from Hawaii, when Michael told her he really was leaving Robin for good. She stopped calling and basically ended our friendship. I can't imagine why she ever thought being friends with me would help her relationship with Michael, but, whatever her reason for needing me, it was no longer there. Also, after months of being really sweet and loving to Talia, she suddenly became one of Talia's worst nightmares.

For months, Talia had spent really fun weekends with Michael and Bronwyn, but she and her dad never had any time alone. Either they were with Bronwyn or Talia was left alone while Michael dated other women. While her dad was with Robin, Talia had been used to having at least a small amount of daddy time, if only because Robin didn't want to be around. Now, there was no alone time at all.

Talia was unhappy about this and told her dad she needed some time alone with him. Michael said that wasn't going to happen. He told her his time was too valuable, and she and Bronwyn would have to share what little time he had. That ripped Talia's heart out. When she came home, she couldn't stop crying.

It broke my heart. I let Michael know that he was absolutely wrong in the way he had spoken to Talia, and he needed to reevaluate the situation. If Bronwyn couldn't allow him some time alone with Talia, then she wasn't the one to be in Talia's life.

Bronwyn found out about my discussion with Michael— Michael told her, of course. When I ran into her at breakfast one day, she decided it was her job to tell me that Talia was a spoiled little brat. Bronwyn said *she* was in Michael's life now, and Talia would have to get over it—she wouldn't have alone time with her dad any more.

Wow, was I blown away! I couldn't believe she had the nerve to tell me that. I also couldn't believe that she, as a mom, didn't understand the importance of Talia's alone time with her dad. But once I stood back and looked at her life, I realized she was incapable of understanding the importance of the father figure in children's lives. While her own family was living in France, she had taken her son away from his father to go live with one of her husband's friends in the US! She also had tried to take her daughter away from her father, as you'll recall.

After that brief encounter with Bronwyn at the coffee shop, I let Michael know what she had said, and I told him she wasn't good for him or for Talia. I actually told him Robin was better than Bronwyn. That tells you something about Bronwyn!

A serious conflict between Talia and her dad arose soon after the coffee shop conversation. Michael had told Talia he was going to take her to Panama for a nice vacation, just the two of them, now that he was done with Bronwyn and Robin. Talia was extremely excited. She asked her dad, "Are you sure Bronwyn isn't going?" He said, "No, she isn't."

Well, just a few days before they were supposed to leave, Bronwyn's son instant-messaged Talia and told her how excited he was about the trip. Talia was stunned. She came to me upset, not knowing what to do. I told her she should call her father and ask him, directly, who was going on the trip.

Talia dialed her dad. She asked him, "Dad, are Brownyn and her kids going to Panama with us?" He said yes. She broke down in tears. She couldn't speak. She reminded him he had promised it would just be the two of them. He then told her she didn't know what she was talking about. Talia said he was lying to her, and he replied that it was she who was lying to him!

She dropped the phone. I picked it up. I told Michael he was more than a jerk for doing that to his daughter. He then proceeded to make up a lot of excuses about not wanting to disappoint Bronwyn's kids. *What about your own daughter!* Well, after I talked with Talia for a long time, she decided to go on the trip. She knew full well that her father had lied to her, but hoped he could redeem himself.

That didn't happen. In fact, the trip was torture for Talia. Bronwyn was emotionally abusive to her the entire time, and Michael did nothing to stop it. When Talia came home and told me some of the things Bronwyn had said to her, I wanted to strangle Bronwyn.

After learning she couldn't trust her father at all, Talia was fed up with Michael and his lies. But they didn't stop, even after Talia told him she didn't believe a word he said!

For a couple of months Michael continued to go out with Bronwyn sporadically. During that time he kept telling Talia how crazy Bronwyn was. He said he wasn't going to see her any more. Then, out of the blue, Bronwyn moved into Michael's house—with her kids! Without giving any notice to Talia, Michael just had her move in.

At that time Bronwyn's ex-husband was suing her for full custody of their daughter. I really believe Bronwyn had convinced Michael to let her move in with him as a way of trying to keep her daughter. Talia, having listened to all of Michael's reasons for breaking up with Bronwyn, was definitely confused when Bronwyn moved in.

Some of the reasons Michael had given for dumping Bronwyn were that she was insane, she wasn't smart, she was a terrible mother, and she was a slob. He even told Talia that in some instances Bronwyn had stalked him. When Michael called to warn me about Bronwyn's behavior and told me to watch out, I let Talia's school know that she was never to go home with Bronwyn. After all that, it was very strange when Michael turned around and had Bronwyn move in with him. No wonder Talia was confused!

It turned out the move into Michael's house was just to help Bronwyn keep her daughter, but it didn't work. After a hearing in San Francisco, the judge awarded full custody of her daughter to the father! The judge saw what a bad mother Bronwyn was. I was subpoenaed by her ex-husband and had to testify to things I had seen or heard. It put me in a difficult spot, but I wasn't going to lie. On the morning of my deposition Michael called and asked me not to tell the truth. I told him I wouldn't do that. I actually believe the judge made the right decision.

Needless to say, all this conflict put a lot of pressure on Talia. She was confused and upset and needed to work through these feelings. She asked me for help, but I knew it would be best for her to deal with Michael directly. I told Talia that if her dad was saying or doing something that hurt her or bothered her, she should tell him how she felt and what he was doing to hurt her.

Talia said she couldn't talk to him; he scared her. I told her the next-best thing would be to write him letters. This might even be better because she could put down her feelings and he wouldn't misinterpret them, as he might in a conversation. I took Talia to a therapist, who told her the same thing. Writing letters would help her tell him what was on her mind, and it would also help her to process her feelings.

So Talia began writing her dad letters. By now it was fall of 2007. Michael had finally broken up with Bronwyn, and she had moved back up north, where she could be with her daughter. Michael's marriage to Robin was over, and he was alone. Though Talia didn't spend a lot of time with her father from the fall of 2007 until that last trip in December, it was enough to give her a chance to be alone with him without the interference of others.

By the end of 2007, Talia was doing so well in her horse show-ing that she was number one in most of her divisions and associations. We spent every weekend away at the final shows of the season. Michael actually made time to take Talia to one of these final shows. I was happy to have her go with him. I wanted her to feel loved and appreciated by her dad.

Around November of 2007, one of the horses Talia had always wanted, Ooh La la, was for sale. It happened that Michael had owned this horse a few years earlier, and Robin had ridden her. Michael had taken advantage of this horse's winning status and sold her. Talia was very upset that La La was sold because she was hoping to grow into this horse. But when Talia told her dad she wanted to keep La La to ride later, Robin told her she would never ride La La, ever. Talk about being mean to a child!

Well, after Robin was out of Talia's life, La La became available, and Talia's trainer brought her in for Talia to try. It was an amazing fit. There was no doubt that Talia and La La would do wonders in the following year's show season. That November, the trainer was able to convince Michael to buy La La back for Talia. Somehow the timing was right, the stars were aligned, and he said OK! I think he was feeling guilty for all he had put Talia through over the years, especially the previous year. So, without Talia's knowledge, he bought this horse.

Talia was showing La La at the Santa Barbara National Horse Show over Thanksgiving when the purchase was finalized. She thought she was riding La La for the current owner. Talia had no idea her dad was buying her La La; in fact, he almost didn't. It seems he changed his mind one hour before he was due to surprise Talia with her. But it worked out. The trainer was able to convince Michael to move forward with the purchase.

Talia had just finished riding La La in one class and was waiting for her next class to begin. All of a sudden the judge announced over the loudspeaker that he wanted Talia to come into the middle of the ring. She quickly looked over and saw Michael with the judge. She thought, *Oh my God, what did my dad do? He must have pissed off the judge, and now he is kicking me out of the show!* She was so nervous!

But she did as the judge requested and rode right into the middle of the ring. Then her dad walked out and the judge announced, "Talia, happy birthday. Your dad just bought you Ooh La La. The horse you are on is now yours!" She was so over-joyed and surprised that she broke down in tears. It was such an emotional moment that even Michael had tears in his eyes. Never before had he done anything for Talia without an ulterior motive. This was the first time he had ever done anything strictly for her happiness. She was overjoyed, and so was he. I am so grateful that his one and only altruistic act for Talia was so spectacular. It was one of her last memories on earth.

PART THREE
THE TRIAL

CHAPTER FIFTEEN

AFTERSHOCKS

As I mentioned earlier, when I got home from Panama, I wasn't just hit with the shock of being back in Santa Barbara without Talia—my financial world was also about to explode.

My entire life had been devoted to raising Talia. It didn't work out well when I tried to work outside the home, and for Talia's sake I dropped the idea of having a job and remained a stay-at-home mom. I was very lucky to be able to do this. Most single mothers have to struggle to make enough money to care for their children, but it was different for me.

Once Michael realized he was going to have to support Talia and me—after the judge threatened to throw him in jail for non-payment of support—his payments to me were always on time. In the beginning I was receiving both spousal and child support, but there came a time when I willingly gave up spousal support altogether.

Michael had bought me out of Transoft. Without going into the details of that transaction, I will say that he got a smoking deal. I had no choice but to sell him my shares for pennies on the dollar; I needed the money. I received the first of two lump sum payments at the signing of the deal; the second half was due at a later date.

But when it came time for Michael to pay the second half, he told me he couldn't afford to pay that sum unless I waived all future spousal support payments. Again, without describing these negotiations with Michael, I finally agreed. I received the rest of my money, and Michael got out of spousal support.

I really didn't care about waiving spousal support—it wasn't that much—as long as Michael continued to pay child support.

Over the years Michael's income grew by leaps and bounds. He put together huge deals. Right after he bought me out of Transoft, he sold it to Hewlett Packard for about $50 million. Then he ran another company called eGroups, which he sold to Yahoo for close to $500 million.

As he made more money, he started to live much more grandly. He bought islands (the islands I mentioned earlier), he bought jets, and he bought a ranch of nearly 1,400 acres, on which he was building a huge house, multiple guesthouses, and an equestrian facility. Talia was lucky to get to travel with her dad in his jets and limousines. But when Talia came home from her dad's, she came home to a very small house and a mom on a budget.

By then, her riding career was taking off, and she was showing all over California and Arizona. I took her to the shows and had to budget for flights and hotels. There were expensive riding boots and coats to buy. I evaluated the situation and asked Michael for more child support.

Michael, behaving in his usual way, told me no. Actually, he told me, "Tough." You get what you get. He didn't want to acknowledge the fact that I was raising Talia and giving her the best life possible. In fact, he went so far as to tell me that if I couldn't live on what he was already giving me, he would have Talia live with him, and he would hire a nanny.

He didn't understand that raising a child is the most important thing a person can do; all he cared about was how much it cost. I told him I was Talia's mother and I was raising her, no one else. I even spoke to him in his own language by showing that the amount of child support he was paying was practically nothing if broken down to an hourly wage, and that he would have to pay a nanny much more.

The law was very clear about child support, but he chose to ignore the law, as he always did. He wouldn't admit that under the law I was entitled to child support commensurate with his income, and he was unwilling to talk to me about an increase. He was so unreasonable that I had to get help from my lawyers.

Over the years my lawyers and I worked out arrangements with Michael for more child support, and that support was my only income up until the time Talia died. Understandably, I was shocked when I received that e-mail from Bob, telling me now that Talia was dead, there was no requirement to pay child support, so he was not going to continue to send it to me.

But although I was concerned about this, I knew I was a beneficiary on a life insurance policy, and I figured the proceeds would keep me from experiencing a financial breakdown. In fact, Bob knew I was supposed to be a beneficiary on the policy, and after telling me he was cutting off child support, he offered to loan me money to pay my bills until the proceeds came through—using the policy as security, of course. He asked me to sign an agreement guaranteeing repayment of the loan, but before we were able to enter into that agreement, I was hit with another surprise.

It was during one of our negotiations for child support that Michael had contracted to make me a beneficiary of a life insurance policy that would help me in the event of his death. Well, it seems that, in regular Michael fashion, he had breached our court-ordered contract, and removed me as the beneficiary of the life insurance policy. In my place was Robin.

That was wrong! At the time of Michael's death he and Robin were all but finished with their divorce. They had a signed property settlement, and all that was needed to finalize the divorce was to file a final judgment with the court. But Michael hadn't yet taken Robin off the policy. Legally he couldn't remove me as the beneficiary, according to our agreement and the court order. But he had done it anyway.

When I found out what he had done, I immediately asked the insurance company not to disburse the funds; they were under dispute. Then my lawyer filed a declaratory relief action to have the courts decide who would get the proceeds—I, to whom the money was obliged to go by court order, or Robin, whom Michael had illegally substituted as the beneficiary.

Even though Bob had cut me off, I still thought of him as family. It may sound odd that I would feel this way about him, but for me family is family, no matter what, and regardless of all Bob had done to me, he was still Talia's grandfather and Michael's dad. Though I did have my own family and friends to talk to about Talia, I really felt that Bob—and Anne, Michael's mom—were the only ones who could truly relate to the way I was feeling. Especially Bob, with whom I felt more of a bond since we had been in Panama together.

So I would periodically send him an e-mail to see how he was doing and to tell him how I was. In one e-mail message I asked him to meet me for lunch. I wanted to visit with him and tell him some of the messages Talia had sent me via Rebecca, and I also wanted to give him Rebecca's phone number. While in Panama Bob had been very interested in Talia's messages, and he had expressed an interest in speaking to Rebecca himself.

Instead of responding to my invitation with a definite yes, Bob stated that he would only meet with me if it were for personal reasons. He said if I wanted to talk about anything having to do with Panama, I had to speak to his lawyer. Of course, I wanted to talk about Panama and about Talia and Michael being gone, but not in the way he had implied. It seems Bob was thinking about Michael's liability for Talia's death long before I ever did. His qualifications for meeting me for lunch hit me like a ton of bricks.

We did end up meeting, but not for lunch. Bob wanted to meet at the beach and walk and talk, but instead of walking we sat on a bench for just a few minutes. I asked how he was and gave him Rebecca's phone number. He didn't ask me how I was; we sat there in silence. Then he started to tell me that regardless of the really bad takeoff of the plane Talia and Michael had been on, the takeoff wasn't what killed them. It was as if he were try-ing to defend Michael before there was anything to defend—this was before any suits had been filed. In fact, at that time filing a lawsuit wasn't even in the back of my mind.

After Bob finished his monologue, we said goodbye and went our separate ways. It was then that I realized Bob didn't think of me as family at all. I suppose I knew this already from the way he had treated me since "the Call," but now it finally sank in. I was pretty upset. Someone I thought of as family had basically cut me out of his life.

I will say that Anne and her husband, Bill, didn't cut me out as Bob did. They kept in touch with me, at least in the beginning. I let them know what Bob had told me about meeting with him alone, and I informed them about the life insurance policy. They said they didn't agree with the way Bob was handling Michael's estate or me, but they had no control over any of it.

While the argument about the life insurance policy was going on, I started to look back at the events that led to Talia's death. I thought how strange it was that Michael was a very experienced, licensed pilot, yet the plane he had chartered or rented for that flight seemed totally inappropriate because of its insufficient size, weight, and power. It was also incomprehensible that he and the other pilot had flown right into a storm and stayed in the storm instead of turning around. I decided to find out what really happened that day. I hired an aviation law firm to investigate.

What they came up with was unbelievable. After sending people down to Panama, they discovered that the accident had been one hundred percent preventable, that it had been caused by pure negligence on the part of Michael and the other pilot, and that Michael's arrogance and risk-taking behavior had killed Talia. After thinking about these findings, I decided to file a wrongful death action against Michael and his estate.

CHAPTER SIXTEEN

THE TRIAL

The only reason I filed the lawsuit was to get justice. Justice for Talia, whose life was taken, and justice for me for having lost my only child, my amazing Talia, killed by the negligence of her father. It wasn't retribution for Bob's treatment of me after we got back from Panama, and it wasn't about money, as Bob and the Kleins seem to think; those are all separate issues. But I will say that I wish I had not had to file the action.

Bob knew the crash had been Michael's fault. The moment he learned that his son and granddaughter were dead, he told someone it was actually his own fault because he was such a terrible father. He said he hadn't raised Michael right, hadn't given him proper guidance, and Michael had grown up a reckless, selfish, and negligent man whose actions killed his own daughter. I wish Bob had wanted to do something to try to make up for Michael's actions, but instead he told me not to call him. He did the same thing to the Lewises, Frankie's parents. He called them and told them not to call him but to contact his attorney instead.

Bob seemed to be running things totally contrary to the way Michael would have wanted them run. From the moment Michael died, everything he had stood for and worked for was completely turned around. He had wanted to protect and preserve the flora and fauna of the islands and his ranch forever. Talia was his sole heir, the only one he could have relied on to keep his properties intact.

Although Michael's estate had the funds to maintain the property forever, Bob decided to sell the islands and the ranch and keep the money, putting an end to Michael's desires and denying an important part of the memory of Michael and Talia. While I have been writing this, the islands have indeed been sold. The ranch is listed, but, with the downturn in the real estate market and the economy, it will be a while before it sells.

At the moment Bob is trying to lease the main house with the equestrian center. It was really hard for me to hear this. That equestrian center was meant for Talia and her trainer. When Talia and Michael died, Bob kicked Talia's trainer out of the barn. With very little notice, she had to find a new place to house Talia's horses, as well as her own and those of her clients. Michael had promised the trainer she could keep her business at the ranch, but Bob didn't care what Michael had planned. He claimed the ranch didn't have the proper permits to allow the trainer to operate there, but that could easily have been fixed. The trainer even offered to take care of the permits, if necessary. But Bob wouldn't have it. He kicked her out.

At the time of his death, Michael was done with Robin. He had set her up in a job at a company he partly owned, and she was literally on her way out of town to start the new job. He wasn't friends with her and wasn't speaking to her. In fact, Robin had told a mutual friend that she hated Michael for what he had done to her and couldn't speak to him any more.

But Robin was great friends with Lynne, who was then Bob's girlfriend, so somehow Bob decided—or possibly was pressured—to hire Robin to help him with Michael's affairs. Now, that was an insult to Michael. Robin wouldn't help her own husband for free when they were married; when she helped Michael out, he had to pay her. He had not let Robin anywhere near his financial affairs for years, and at the time of the crash they were basically divorced.

Now Bob had hired her to be in control of everything Michael had kept her from! And—what a surprise—she didn't work for Bob out of the goodness of her heart. She negotiated a real employment contract with him at a high salary. It was like a soap opera.

On top of that, Michael's personal lawyer, Gary—who, by the way, was my personal lawyer until Michael and I got divorced—was now representing Robin in the life insurance action I had against her. Gary was also representing Michael's estate and Bob in the life insurance action I had against them for Michael's breach of contract with regard to the life insurance policy. Here was one lawyer representing two parties with contrary interests against a third party who had formerly been his client!

You would think Bob would want to get the wrongful death suit out of his hair as soon as possible. You would think he wouldn't want to hear the acts of his son aired in open court, or to have to sit there and listen to the details of the flight that killed his granddaughter. Michael was a daredevil who thought nothing bad would ever happen to him. Throughout his life, both in business and in hobbies, he had always pushed the limits and come out on top. He was blind to all risk, but this time he had guessed wrong and killed himself, and, worse yet, his daughter, *my* daughter.

Instead of negotiating an honorable settlement with me, my former lawyer Gary decided to play hardball. During one of my depositions in the wrongful death suit, he asked me whether Talia was my *meal ticket*. Then he went on to ask question after question about why Talia hated Robin so much. Had I badmouthed Robin to Talia, causing her to hate Robin? Of course I hadn't, but Talia's feelings toward Robin were not the issue. Robin wasn't an issue in the entire wrongful death suit, so why press the point?

Gary's questions about Robin had no bearing on the case; however, they seemed to have some personal importance to him. No one I talk to can understand Gary's concern for Robin in the context of the case. The only explanation we can find is that he had something more than an attorney-client relationship with her. Of course, we don't have proof; we are surmising this based on his actions.

Even before the trial started, Bob seemed to be totally incapable of thinking for himself. His lawyers were running all over the place racking up fees from Michael's estate, and he let it happen. It was so obvious that Bob was being misled with regard to my wrongful death suit that the judge we used during a pretrial mediation for the suit told Bob, in front of his lawyers and mine, that he, Bob, was the one who had to make the final decision. He would have to live with the consequences of this suit, and the final decision whether to settle the case was *his alone.*

The judge urged him to stand up and do what was right. But Bob let Gary control him. On top of it all, the lawyers for Michael's personal liability insurance company were pulling Bob's strings. All they cared about were the fees they could rack up defending Michael's estate against negligence claims. But even though all these lawyers were telling him not to settle, Bob still had the power to do what was right. And he didn't.

Instead of taking the judge's statement to heart, Bob remained oblivious to the truth about his son's liability. As we neared our trial date, Gary and the other defense lawyers made me the most insulting settlement offers imaginable. It felt as if their goal was to use my daughter's death to rip my heart out. I won't mention the amount they offered me to settle—settlement discussions are confidential—but you, the reader, would have been appalled.

As the first day of jury selection neared, I was getting excited. Nervous too, because I wasn't looking forward to having Talia's last day reenacted over and over, or hearing and seeing the details of the crash that killed her. But I was looking forward to getting the truth out there. I really wanted the world to know how Michael's actions and inactions had led to Talia's death. I wanted the world to know how he treated me throughout our life together, and how his risk-taking attitude had led to the crash. I also wanted the world to hear about how Michael's dad, Talia's grandfather, treated me.

No one could believe it when I described Bob's heartlessness after the crash. Nor could people understand exactly why he was being so cruel to me. They would ask me if he and I had gotten along before, or whether I had ever done anything to anger him, but I could come up with nothing.

However, I did know Michael, and I knew it was his M.O. to say anything to anyone in order to justify his actions or inactions. He would tell an outright lie about an incident or a person if that would further his agenda. Knowing this, I surmised that Michael must have spent the years leading up to his death badmouthing me to his dad and others in his life in order to justify his behavior toward me. What else could it have been?

I figured he made up some lies about my being a bitch, or psychotic, or a bad mom, in order to justify the way he left our marriage. He wasn't man enough to just admit he wanted a divorce;

he had to make me look bad. Also, I know from talking to various people in his life that he always complained about paying me support. He even complained about having to spend his weekends with Talia. I began to put together a hypothesis about why Bob was so mean to me. It seems I was correct in my theory, too.

It wasn't Bob who confirmed that Michael had tainted people's opinions of me over the years; it was Michael himself. During a number of sessions with a medium who was talking to Talia and Michael for me, Michael apologized profusely to me. He told me he was sorry for the way he treated me. He also said that since his death he had been trying to get through to his dad and other members of his family, to point them in the direction of being fair to me, but that he couldn't break through their hard heads.

Of course, he couldn't break through to them because he had done such a good job of badmouthing me to them over the years. Michael, in spirit, has admitted to lying about me to his dad and others to defend his own actions. He said he lied so much that they now think of me as an evil person and have no sympathetic feelings for me at all. Hearing Michael's apologies has helped me a great deal in grieving for him. I have forgiven him for his treatment of me during his lifetime, but that doesn't change the way I've been treated by his dad and by Michael's lawyers since Michael's death.

I'm not going to recount every moment of the trial, but I will talk about some of the more interesting portions.

First of all, we—my lawyers and the Lewises' lawyers—never disputed that the official pilot of the small plane, Edwin Lasso, was also responsible for the crash. But Michael's lawyers spent ninety percent of their time trying to convince the jury that Edwin was the *sole* cause of the crash. Of course, it was their duty to defend Michael's actions to the best of their ability, but come on. It was abundantly clear that Michael had breached his duty to protect Talia and Frankie *well before the day of that final flight.*

You see, Michael had originally booked Talia, Frankie, and himself on a flight with Rudolfo—the main charter pilot Michael had used to transport guests of the islands—in October 2007, more than two months before that final trip. For some reason— we believe it was the cost—Michael decided not to use Rudolfo but to hire another pilot, Marvin, whose services were half the price. Michael made this decision even though he had heard from one of his sources that Marvin was incompetent to land at the islands.

We read this in an email we received during discovery in the wrongful death case. Corresponding with his assistant to get confirmation of his flight plans, Michael instructed her to book the flight with Marvin for himself and the girls despite Marvin's lack of skill. Michael explained to her that he didn't have to worry about Marvin's skills because Marvin would be landing solo when he came to pick them up at the islands. It was very clear to me that Michael himself was going to fly them off the island and to their destination. He needed the pilot only to get the plane to him at the islands. But this was never proved.

On the day of the flight, Marvin didn't even show up. A totally unknown pilot, Edwin Lasso, is the one who came to fly Talia, Frankie, and Michael off the islands. Michael accepted him without questioning his qualifications, who he was, or why he was there instead of Marvin. This just gives more credibility to my theory that Michael was willing to accept Marvin despite his reputation for incompetence, then take this unknown pilot instead, because Michael himself intended to do the flying from the islands to Volcan. He didn't care who brought him the plane because he was planning to take control once he got on board himself.

Before and during trial, my attorneys had shown that Michael had piloted himself in Panama on numerous occasions. He had even flown to Volcan and around that area. Michael's lawyers tried to claim that Michael had never been at the controls of any plane while in Panama, but we produced Michael's logbooks, which showed his piloting experience in Panama.

Michael's lawyers said they were incorrect—but the logbooks speak for themselves. Either Michael did in fact fly in Panama, as the logbooks proved, or he had made fraudulent entries in his logbooks to reflect flights he had not flown. Either way, it didn't reflect well on him.

Weather was another important fact in the trial. The weather in Panama had been horrible. Period. Not one of the defense experts could dispute that. Even the recordings of the pilot and the control tower showed that the plane was flying in bad weather and heading into a storm. The pilots couldn't see. They plainly shouldn't have been in the sky. Any reasonable and prudent person, especially a pilot, should have turned around and gone back to clear skies and landed.

Michael was in control of that plane, and whether or not he was handling the actual controls, he was in control of the pilot in command. *Every* person on that witness stand—our witnesses and the defense witnesses—said that the plane shouldn't have been flying. *All* the witnesses said they would have told the pilot to turn around and land. Michael had never given up in his entire life—he had beaten all the odds, and his blindness to risk is what kept him from acting reasonably. That is what killed my daughter. Plain and simple.

Besides having to sit through all the expert witnesses, who were talking about the weather, the duties of pilots, and so on, I myself was put through hell by Gary while on the stand.

The Trial

I had to testify in court, of course. I wanted to, and I needed to. I wanted to let the jury know, and the world as well, how wonderful Talia was as a person, a daughter, and a companion, and that she was my life. My attorney, Marc, took me through life with Talia in a very respectful manner. I was nervous and emotional, but I was OK up to that point. When it was time for my cross-examination by the defense, Gary decided it was his job not only to try to discredit me as a person but to portray me as a bad mother.

He started in with his questions straight out, without even the slightest "I'm sorry for your loss." I shouldn't have been surprised because not once during the discovery period of the case, or during any mediation, did Gary tell me he was sorry. Here is a man who is a father himself, who has known me for years. Twenty years! He knew me before I was pregnant and while I was pregnant, and he knew Talia. Yes, he had worked against me in the past, taking Michael's side during the divorce and helping him virtually steal my part of the company from me, but I expected him to at least have some compassion for me as a mom. He had none.

Every chance he could, Gary turned my devotion to Talia against me. He wanted to make it look as if Talia and I had a neurotic relationship. He tried to prove that it was unhealthy and that I had been harming Talia in some way. This didn't work. His implications were squelched by the testimony of my witnesses, who in no uncertain terms spoke about their envy of my relationship with Talia. Their testimony bore out that though we were so close, Talia was truly a wonderful and independent child.

Gary also tried to make it look like all I cared about was money, as if I didn't care about Talia at all. Both during my deposition and while I was on the stand in court, he tried to twist a question I had asked the coroner in Panama to make it appear that I was asking a government official to commit fraud.

Nothing could be further from the truth. When I tried to explain to him and the court why I had asked the coroner about Talia's time of death—I needed to know she didn't suffer—he turned the answer around and actually said to me, "Do you not know what a broken neck is?" You see, Talia died of a broken neck. That was cruel. But that is Gary.

This happened on the second day of my deposition, in one of the final questions at the end of the day. My conversation with the coroner in Panama was blown out of proportion and warped to such an extent that I'm going to explain it in more detail than it deserves. But I want the truth of this conversation out there. It wasn't what Gary tried to make it out to be. And while I honestly don't remember in detail everything that happened at the coroner's, I do remember bits and pieces. And my brother and father reminded me of what they had told me.

On that day I was in shock over Talia being dead, I was freaked out about going to see her lifeless body and saying goodbye to her forever, and I was frustrated that information was being withheld from me. Right before going to the coroner's office to see Talia for the last time, I got into an argument with Lynne, Bob's then girlfriend, in the driveway of Linda's house. (You may recall that incident from Chapter 5.) Lynne and Bob had greatly upset me, first by not wanting me to go to the coroner's office and then by trying to prevent my family from going there with me.

In addition, I had been totally cut off from all decisions about Talia. Bob told me that he and his friend Jim W. had already picked out the caskets for Talia and Michael and had arranged for autopsies. I didn't want an autopsy for Talia, but Bob and Jim told me it was required in Panama. I believed them and still do, but the point is, I wasn't consulted about anything.

On top of everything, Jim W. had been handling all the paperwork surrounding the deaths and somehow was able to get the coroner to work late into the night to perform the autopsies of Talia and Michael, which I was told she never, ever does. He also arranged for their bodies to be transported to Panama City that night, right after the autopsies, to be cremated in the early morning. That is never done. In Panama it normally takes weeks to complete this process and get permission to take the remains out of the country.

Right after the fight in the driveway, my dad told me to be sure to find out what time Talia had died. He said it was important. He said I couldn't trust Michael's family—he knew this from observing their treatment of me in Panama and from my history with Michael. Right before I went in to see Talia and say goodbye to her, my brother also told me not to trust Michael's family. He said it was important from the aspect of life insurance, knowing that the Kleins would somehow try to cheat me.

Not only had my father and brother witnessed the Kleins' treatment of me in Panama, they had been supportive throughout my life with Michael and knew how he had repeatedly mistreated me and cheated me. They were worried that somehow the Kleins would interfere with my rights as Talia's mom, and they were worried about the insurance proceeds. They were right to be worried. I never did receive the insurance proceeds to which I was legally entitled.

After I saw Talia at the coroner's and was on my way out, I did what my dad and brother had told me to do. I stopped to talk to the coroner herself. I simply asked her how Talia died. I needed to know she had not suffered, and I asked the coroner if she had died before or after Michael. I told her not to just put the same time down for both of them, but to put down the actual time of death. If Talia died after Michael, I asked her to please put that down.

In no way did I tell her to lie. In no way did I ask her to commit fraud. I simply asked her *if* Talia had died before or after her father. It had nothing to do with money; I just wanted the truth. Even if Michael had died first, Talia would have had to live a month after his death and be at least 18 years old to inherit his estate. There was no way I could inherit Michael's money.

But that was the discussion with the coroner that gave Gary ammo to try to make me look as if I didn't care about my daughter's death, as if all I cared about was money. Though he tried very hard to try to make me look bad, and he succeeded on some level in some people's minds, I'm sure anyone with any intelligence could see through this.

First of all, from the very beginning of this part of my deposition I admitted I had spoken to the coroner, that I was worried about insurance money. I never lied. I didn't try to hide anything.

More important, the defense lawyers had deposed everyone they could get their hands on in Panama—but not the coroner. They even brought witnesses in from Panama for the trial in Santa Barbara—but not the coroner. If in fact I had said or done what they were accusing me of—if I had committed fraud or tried to pressure a government official—they would have deposed the coroner and brought her to the trial. They would have wanted the jury to hear it straight from her mouth. The reason they didn't bring her in or depose her is that when they met with her, she didn't say what they wanted her to say. She told them what had really happened: that I had asked an innocent question of her. If they had put her on the stand, she would have discredited them. The truth would have hurt them. But unfortunately, their innuendo worked.

After questioning me about the coroner, Gary asked me why I had flown home from Panama, leaving Bob with the job of taking care of Talia and her funeral arrangements. As if I would have done that! I was in Panama when Bob made those arrangements without my consent. I didn't leave him to do it for me; I was actually angry that I had been left out of the planning.

My answer seemed to come as a surprise: "I brought my daughter's ashes home in my backpack." Gary was stunned. He said, "What—what do you mean? Where did you get the ashes?" As if I were lying. I then started to tell him that I got the ashes from . . . and I couldn't think of the word *crematorium.* I said, ". . . from that place . . . in Panama City." That seemed to shut him up.

I was holding up all right until Gary and my lawyers had a sidebar (a private discussion with the judge), at which time I totally broke down on the stand. It was horrible.

After I was off the stand, I was more than relieved. But I still had to sit through a few more defense witnesses, whose sole purpose was to try to make Michael look like a wonderful, dedicated father and me a lying, heartless mother.

Bob Klein got on the stand and went into how Michael was a good kid, never did drugs, was responsible, and so on, and how he didn't think of Michael as special—meaning more brilliant than any other child. Then he said he didn't think I was a good mother, implying that I overindulged Talia by traveling with her to Los Angeles to go shopping and to visit the chiropractor. He didn't realize that I was taking her to Los Angeles to see the same chiropractor and visit the same stores I had been going to since I was fifteen years old.

My attorney asked Bob if he realized that Michael gave Talia horses, built her a barn, and traveled with her in private jets, showing that I wasn't the only parent who "spoiled" Talia, if in fact that were the case. Michael did that on a much grander scale. Bob admitted Michael did all of these things for Talia but kept pushing the fact that Michael loved Talia more than anything and that she felt the same way toward him.

After my attorney acknowledged to Bob that it was true there was great love between Michael and Talia, despite the little time they spent together, he then asked, "Don't you think that Talia loved her mom at least that amount, and Kim, Talia, since they were together more?" That shut Bob up. He realized he had just proved how much love Talia and I shared for each other.

I won't go into all of the testimony, but I will add that Linda, Michael's sister, was caught lying on the stand. In her deposition she had acknowledged that Talia had gotten sick while in the Darien Province in Panama with Michael, but on the stand she said Talia hadn't been sick at all. Not a sign of sickness. This was important because it showed, one, that she had lied; two, that she was covering up for Michael's irresponsible behavior in taking Talia to such a dangerous place; and, three, that he didn't care for her health properly while they were away.

Then Robin got on the stand. She tried to come off as a kind, devoted stepmother whose husband was a great dad and a man who didn't know much about planes, but, during cross-examination by my attorney, she wasn't able to hide her coldness. With her calculated answers, her true self emerged.

She was caught covering up for Michael's knowledge of aviation and covering up for her and Michael's lack of child supervision when Talia stayed with them at the ranch, before the house was built. She tried to say that the tiny separate room in which they made Talia sleep was right next to their room, but actually it wasn't close at all. She and Gary showed a photo of the place, trying to make the jury think the building she and Michael lived in was a modest "love shack," not a large house. Talia's little room wasn't even in the photo. Robin said the room was just outside the photo frame, but that wasn't true. If it had been that close, they would have shown it.

Talia was five and six years old, sleeping alone in a room detached from the rest of the building. She had to walk outside to go to the bathroom. And this was up in the hills, where bears and mountain lions are seen on a daily basis. But little did I know that having Talia sleep in her own room at the ranch, separate and distant from Michael's, wasn't the only unbelievable risk Michael took with Talia's safety.

While I was sitting in the courtroom, listening to various witnesses speak about the very special relationship Talia and I had, one of Talia's close friends, Caroline, took the stand, and what I heard floored me. Caroline had gone to Panama with Talia and Michael for the holidays a couple of years before the accident. When they arrived in Panama City, they stayed overnight, planning to head over to the islands the next day.

That night, Michael allowed Talia and Caroline to go shopping and walking around Panama City *alone,* while he stayed at the hotel and socialized with his girlfriend. Talia was around ten years old! The girls could have been hurt, kidnapped, anything. Caroline also testified that when they stayed on one of the islands, she and Talia had slept in a cabin by themselves. Under the right circumstances, that wouldn't have been such a big deal, but this cabin was on a different island than Michael's cabin!

To get over to the main island for meals and activities, the girls had to call for a boat to pick them up. Worse yet, the phone in their cabin stopped working, and to call for the boat Talia had to use her cell phone to call her dad, who then notified the boat guy to pick them up.

What was he thinking? Anything could have happened. First off, who was this boat guy? Second, the islands are along the exact route used by Colombian drug traffickers on their way up the coast to America. I nearly fainted when I heard all this in the courtroom.

Well, as we neared the end of the trial, I was more than confident that Michael would be found negligent and liable for the death of Talia. All our witnesses showed that though Michael wasn't the official pilot in command, he too had a duty to turn around, get that plane out of the weather, and land safely. He also had a duty to research the pilot's background and not to use a pilot who was flying a plane that wasn't legal for charter. All our cross-examinations proved that every one of the defense witnesses either wouldn't have taken that flight at all or would have told the pilot to turn around. We had clearly proved Michael was at fault.

Once all the testimony was in, it was time for closing arguments from both sides. My attorney did an amazing job, showing how Michael had breached his duty of care and reminding the jury of exactly what I had lost. Everything. My life.

The defense attorneys then started their closing arguments. One of them, named Peter, the attorney for Michael's liability insurance company, started with his closing argument on liability. He said the weather had not been bad, it was only the last two minutes of the flight that mattered, and it was only because Lasso, the pilot in command, took a left turn too soon that they crashed. Instead of turning left to go around the mountain, he said, Lasso made a left turn into a box canyon. That was the only mistake the pilots made on the flight, he said. Of course, it was his job to convince the jury that the only person liable for the crash was Edwin Lasso.

After Peter's closing, Gary got up for his closing argument regarding damages. His job was to convince the jury to give me very little or nothing. I have to admit he wasn't as mean as he had been when I was on the stand, but he did tell the jury that they shouldn't reward me for having a dead child. He used those exact words: *Don't reward her.*

He then said that if it were he, he would just go out and plant some trees in Talia's memory and be done with it. That was totally insulting. Little did he know, I did plant trees in Talia's name. I also commissioned bronze statues of Talia jumping her horse, to be used as perpetual trophies in Talia's memory in both the Pacific Coast Horse Show Association and the Northern California Hunter Jumper Associations. I'm planning to fund numerous animal welfare charities in Talia's name.

But none of these things relieve the pain of losing Talia. None of them make up for Michael having killed Talia. None of this will bring my daughter back to me.

After the closing arguments were over, the judge closed the trial and told the jury the case was now in their hands. Wow, I was nervous. I knew I was going to win—I had no doubt because I knew Michael and his pattern of behavior so well—but I was still nervous.

The judge let the jury have the case on Friday around 11:30 a.m. They had a half-day on Friday to deliberate, and then they would have three days off for the Labor Day weekend before starting up again.

Those three days were horrible. I couldn't wait for the jury to reconvene and to get the verdict in. Tuesday came. I waited until lunch—nothing. Tuesday evening came, when the jury ends for the day at 4:30. Nothing. I had expected it to go faster.

I figured the jurors were taking their time deciding the percentage of liability to allocate to Lasso and to Michael, and also the amount of damages they would award me. I was so sure, deeply sure, that they would find Michael at least fifty percent liable, if not more, and that they would find Michael had control over Lasso, making Michael responsible for Lasso's negligence, too.

Wednesday morning came. Today was the day—I knew it. But it was already 11:30, and nothing. I decided to leave my house and go down to the hotel where my lawyers were staying to meet them for lunch. I got there a bit before court let out for lunch, so I made a telephone call. When I got off that call, I looked at my phone and saw a text message from Stuart, one of my lawyers. We had a verdict. He was telling me to get to the courthouse.

I basically had ten minutes to get to court. The judge gives you very little time before reading the verdict. I leaped up from my chair and hurried out the door and down the street. It was right then that I started to feel sick. I could hardly breathe. I was really nervous. I was nearly running down the street, trying to get to the court before the verdict was read. As I neared the courthouse steps I couldn't breathe. I tried to compose myself, and then I slowly opened the courtroom door.

As I opened the door I saw the judge standing up, facing the jury box, holding the verdict form in his hands. All I heard was, "Michael Klein wasn't negligent." *What? What did I hear? Did I hear right?* I thought the judge was reading through the questions, not reading the answers. No way could that be the verdict. Michael *not* negligent?

I walked over to my side of the courtroom. The only person sitting there was one of my attorneys' assistants. I sat down next to him. He looked at me. I looked back. *What? Are you kidding me?* He had a very disturbed expression on his face. I felt my heart sink. As I looked at him I put my sunglasses over my eyes and stared at the judge. I couldn't look at the jury. I wasn't sure what I was hearing. *Not negligent? Impossible.*

But as I sat there, I realized that was in fact the verdict. The jury had not found Michael negligent even the slightest bit. I held back my tears. I didn't want to cry. As the jury was polled, asked who voted this way or that, there were three jurors who had voted against the grain. Those three felt Michael was in fact negligent, as he was!

When the judge was finished with the jury, he thanked them for their service and dismissed them. They all filed out—walked right by me without so much as a glance. Then one of the men jurors came up to me. He was one who felt Michael was negligent. He leaned down, took my hand, and told me he was really, really sorry. Truly sorry. He left. Then the other man among the three came up, and he too told me he was sorry. He had tears in his eyes. I thanked him. Then the third juror, a woman, came up to me. She had red, swollen eyes. She had been crying and was still crying. She told me she didn't know what to say. She was so upset and was so, so sorry. We both started to cry. I thanked her as well.

As soon as I thought the courtroom was empty, I looked up to my left, and Bob was standing there. As I saw him, he told me that he was very sorry. I looked away. I then started to cry and couldn't stop. He left. Sorry. How could he tell me he was sorry? He had had the ability to do the right thing from day one. To sit here now and tell me he was sorry was useless and meaningless.

As I was walking out of the courtroom, I noticed two of the jurors who were for me in the deliberating room. I went in. I thanked them again, and we all started to cry. Then I asked them what had happened.

It seems there had been one juror who had made it his mission to fight to prove Michael wasn't negligent. They told me he kept pressing the point that no one knows what happened *in the plane*. Well, what happened in the plane is not the issue. The issue is that they were flying that plane in the first place, the plane flew into and stayed in the bad weather, and it crashed. What the pilot and Michael were talking about in the plane wasn't an issue. Michael was negligent before they even boarded the plane, and he became more and more negligent as the flight continued.

For one man to work so hard to disprove negligence makes me wonder why. We will never really know what motivated him to work for the defense, but that was what he was doing. He put his heart and soul into working for the defense. And he beat everyone down. The worst part is that the last juror to be beaten down said she just gave in. If she had stood her ground, then it would have been a hung jury, and that would have been great, compared to a complete loss.

As I walked away from the courthouse to meet with my attorneys, I came to the corner, and Bob was standing there. He looked at me, and I looked at him. Neither of us said anything, though I know we both wanted to.

When I told my friend G. what had happened, he was shocked. He asked, "Was the jury there?" His question hit home. The verdict was so contrary to the evidence it was as if the jury were not even there at the trial. Their minds not there, their hearts not there. Not in the same courtroom. So many meanings to this simple statement.

After the verdict was read and I was back at the hotel where my attorneys were staying during trial, I asked one of my lawyers what had happened. He said they didn't know. They did know that the judge was very upset about the verdict as well. They said that after the verdict, in chambers, he told them he thought we should have won, assigning at least 40 percent of the liability to Michael.

My lawyer told me the judge said he didn't know what happened, either. Well, with that information I felt there might be a good chance the judge would, on our motion, grant us a judgment notwithstanding the verdict—when the judge overturns the jury's decision and makes a new ruling. Why would he not? He didn't agree with them; he had the right to change the verdict.

I knew if he did that, the defense would appeal, but I didn't care because at least I would have justice for Talia. I would have a verdict that said yes, Michael was negligent and his negligence killed Talia. But without a judgment notwithstanding the verdict, we had a total loss, and we would be the ones appealing. That is exactly what happened.

A few weeks after the trial, my lawyers filed a motion for judgment notwithstanding the verdict. They also filed a motion for a new trial. The defense filed a motion demanding that I pay the costs associated with the defense. I wasn't surprised they did this, because there is a statute that allows the winning side to file a motion for costs if they had made an offer to settle that was rejected. We had rejected the Kleins' insulting lowball offer before we went to trial, and that opened the door to their filing a motion to get me to pay their costs. They had been heartless since day one.

All of our motions were overruled. No new trial and no judgment notwithstanding the verdict. The defense's motion for costs was granted. Now, basically, I'm paying them for Michael killing Talia. Didn't they hurt me enough by taking my daughter, ripping my heart out? Now I have to pay them! Who cares about the statute that allows for this to happen—has anyone ever heard of having a heart?

No. Not Bob, nor anyone remotely close to Michael. They go for blood. Always. On top of all of this, I don't understand why the judge didn't grant our motion notwithstanding the verdict. He didn't agree with the verdict after the trial, so why not grant this? What changed for him? I can't help but wonder exactly what happened to change his mind between the jury verdict, when the judge was surprised about my loss, and the time of our motion.

As I write this, we are getting ready to file our appeal. One of the most significant appealable mistakes of this case is that the judge allowed the defense to enter evidence from after the accident. It is extremely clear under the law that post-death evidence is not admissible in a wrongful death suit. The judge not only allowed the defense to enter all sorts of post-death statements, he didn't allow our side to make the proper counterarguments to defeat the improperly admitted information. He slammed us twice. He let it in and let it go undisputed. That was extremely prejudicial.

Then he used that improperly admitted information in his ruling granting the defense motion to force me to pay costs, and, to top it off, he denied our motion for a new trial. That is totally unfair, against the word of the law, and totally appealable.

Who knows what will happen? I do know one thing. Regardless of what the appeals court decides, I know, Bob knows, and anyone who knew Michael knows that Michael was in fact negligent, and his negligence is what killed my daughter. All I want is for one official person to say that Michael killed Talia, to get the justice that Talia's life deserves.

PART FOUR
TALIA

Chapter Seventeen

Tell My Mom I'm Okay

What gives me the strength to deal with Bob and the whole Klein contingent during this lawsuit, and at the same time try to get on with my life without Talia in it? How am I able to deal with the reality that my daughter is not with me any more?

It's strange. During this most devastating time of my life, I actually have a great deal of peace. It may seem impossible to understand, but it's really easy when you realize that I get through my days and nights because I know that Talia is with me, and is always going to be with me.

I don't mean this in the traditional religious way—I don't mean she's in heaven, watching over me. I mean it in a deep, factual, no-doubt-about-it, beyond-belief way. For me, Talia is not dead. She's alive and living a life even more amazing than the one she had with me.

How do I know? Because she has told me. She has also told my mom, my friends, her friends, anyone who has tried to contact her and those whom she has been able to contact.

No, I'm not crazy. What I'm talking about is that I'm able to communicate with Talia through people whose minds are open and clear. They are able to see and hear those who have "died" while here in our world but whose consciousness continues to be alive in another dimension.

I believe we're all capable of this communication but don't realize it. In fact, Talia has said this herself: we're all capable of communicating with the spirits—it's just that we don't believe, for various reasons. We may have been told while growing up that it was evil to communicate with spirits, or perhaps our religious leaders made us think the only way to heaven was through themselves. Whatever the reason, even if people believe in the spirit world, they don't believe they're capable of communicating with it. Yet as I write this, I myself am learning to communicate with Talia.

I didn't always believe that we could communicate with spirits, or that the soul continues to live after the body dies. I used to believe nothing happened after you died. But that has changed. Changed because of Talia's communications from the "afterlife."

> *Tell my mom I'm OK.*
> *Talia?*
> *Yes, tell my mom I'm OK.*
> *OK, I will when I see her.*
> *TELL MY MOM I'M OK!*
> *I will, I promise!*

That was it—or so I thought at the time. What sounded like an everyday message from a daughter to her mother really was not so everyday. You see, Talia made that statement to my friend G. on January 23, 2008, while he was on the way to her memorial service. She said it a month *after* she died.

Since I didn't believe in the spirit world, why would I ever believe that those words, "Tell my mom I'm OK," were actually from Talia? It would have been much more rational for me to assume my friend had made up that message to help me deal with the overwhelming pain of losing my daughter.

But when G. gave me Talia's message, I knew, deep in my heart, that those were Talia's own words. Yes, they were said to help me, but they were not made up; they were actually Talia's words, said by her, for me.

Who am I? you may be wondering. I'm Kim, Talia's mom. A forty-something, California-raised, well-educated, middle-class woman. I grew up pretty simply, with no particular religious or spiritual rules to live by. I just lived my life my way, rationally and according to my own guidelines, which were pretty basic: Try to treat people well, don't lie, and be happy.

Because I didn't have any set religious or spiritual guidance while growing up, I decided I didn't believe in God—or the spirit world. I was too independent to believe there was one supreme person or entity with a set of rules I was supposed to follow in order to go to heaven when I died. In fact, that idea annoyed me, because I saw so many religious leaders using their position to control the members of their congregations.

I felt that if there was a God, you should be able to pray to that God directly—he wouldn't make it necessary for people to go through an intermediary to get to him. There was no need to pray to a secondary source or confess to a human as God's representative, or do whatever a particular leader said you had to do. Nor did you have to join a church or temple as a means of getting to heaven. You could just be you, live your life, and speak to your God when you wanted to, on your terms.

But though I didn't believe in the God that most people I came in contact with believed in, I didn't shut myself off from the possibility of the existence of God, either. Since the idea of God had not been pounded into me, and until recently I had had no mystical experiences or miracles to show me the existence of God, I had no reason to believe in either the existence or the nonexistence of a God. But I was open to receiving proof of the existence of God or the spirit world. And I did believe in my own instincts, often "just knowing" something, which seemed to imply that I believed there's more to us than our minds.

I labeled myself *agnostic*—not believing but open to proof. I really believe it was this openness that allowed me eventually to see, hear, and experience the evidence I needed to prove that there is in fact a spiritual dimension and a power, a force that some people call God.

So what was it that changed me from not believing to believing? It was just after I really understood that my daughter had been killed that my entire belief system was shattered. I say it happened when I really *understood* that she was killed, not when I first found out, because, as you know from my account of the incidents in Panama, it took a while for me to really know she was gone. Gone from this earth the way I knew her. Once I realized she was in fact "dead," my entire belief system shattered.

This shattering was not like shattering a mirror, whereby when it broke nothing was left. It was like shattering a frosted glass door that, once broken, allowed me to see into a world much more beautiful, perfect, and fulfilling than the world I was living in. From the moment I really understood she was gone, I went from not believing in the spirit world to absolutely believing in it. I knew that the messages Talia was sending me from beyond were from her, and so very real.

It wasn't just the words "Tell my mom I'm OK" in themselves that changed me from a non-believer to a believer. From the very moment I realized Talia was "dead," I began receiving messages from her through various sources, which built on each other and were confirmed by each other. When looked at both individually and as a whole, these proved to me that not only was Talia actually telling people the messages they relayed to me, but, beyond that, those messages were totally, completely, and irrevocably Talia. In fact, it has become clear to me that she is more alive and amazing now than she was with me here on earth.

You may recall Talia's first communication with me, described in Chapter Four, when she touched my wrist. At the same time Rebecca was hearing from Talia that she wanted me to get her bracelet. My first couple of conversations with Rebecca after that were filled with short messages from Talia to me, meant to help me get over the shock of the accident. Here is a little of what Talia said to me through Rebecca. I'll explain their significance as needed.

Talia loves you. She's with her dad.

Talia and her dad stayed at the plane with Frankie to keep her safe until help came. They kept Frankie in a daze to keep her from panicking. They protected Frankie.

Talia said her dad guided Sam to help find the plane.

Talia wants you to get her backpack. She's worried about it.

Talia said she had the best life, a charmed life, and still considers it the same way.

Talia is concerned about the dogs and her male horse; he will be upset with any change.

Talia had two horses, a male and a female. Her male horse, Justinian, is an extremely emotional animal, and he was very attached to her. He reacts to change, so Talia's letting me know that she was concerned about him was significant.

Talia is concerned about her awards and wants you to make sure to get them for her.

Talia had won numerous equestrian awards during the 2007 horse show year, and she was the number one equitation rider in her age group in our region. Talia had been looking forward to going to the awards banquets and receiving her awards in January.

*Tomorrow will be difficult for you. She doesn't want you to look at her this way. She had **no pain.***

The day after I got these messages from Talia, I was to go to the morgue to identify her body and to visit her in the flesh for the last time. No one knew that in the States. Only the members of my family who were with me in Panama knew. It was going to be a very difficult day for me, and in fact it was. I'll never forget the expression on Talia's face, ever. Talia didn't want me to remember her that way, and she was making a point of telling me that.

Talia said you were the best mother and will always be her mom.

Talia is with Stella. All passed family is with her. Stella has her by the arm, and she will be fine; she's there for you.

Stella is my grandmother, who died in 1980. Stella is not a common name, not one to be guessed.

Talia wants photos and music as her memory. Said you know the song.

There is a particular song that was Talia's favorite at the time, and I knew exactly which one it was. Also, Talia had many photos of herself riding that she was very proud of.

Talia wants you to look for the hummingbirds.

The hummingbird message didn't have any significance to me when I first got the message in Panama, but as soon as I got home it did. I started seeing hummingbirds hovering by my office window, looking in, all the time. In one instance it was pouring rain, and this little hummingbird was outside my window. I said out loud, "Talia, is that you? It has to be, because hummingbirds don't usually fly in the rain."

No more than ten minutes after I said that, I went to my back door, and as I was stepping out I saw, placed perfectly on the step, straight and centered, the same hummingbird I had just seen by my window on the other side of the house. It was wet and freshly dead. That was a confirmation from Talia, saying, "Yes, Mom, it's me, and to prove it I'm making a statement!"

Talia told you to get her diary or journal.

Besides the messages above, which I received right after Talia died, there were some remarkable events that further solidified my newfound beliefs. Everyone I knew who was close to Talia and me, or close to Michael, was clamoring for communications with them via Rebecca.

One afternoon I was visiting a friend of mine, and we were talking about my upcoming birthday. I mentioned to her that my mom wanted to receive a message from Talia to find out what Talia wanted her to get me for my birthday. I commented that it would be amazing if Talia told my mom exactly what gift to get me and where to buy it.

My mom called Rebecca and left her request. While waiting for a return call, she started to search the Internet for a gift Talia might want me to have. She found what she thought was the perfect gift, and as she was looking at it on her computer screen, the phone rang. It was Rebecca returning her call. "Talia wants you to get her mom a glass heart." My mom almost died. On the computer screen, at that very moment, was a photo of a glass heart. A pink glass heart.

Some other friends of mine, a married couple, had a phone-in appointment with Rebecca no more than thirty minutes after the conversation I'd had about my birthday. During this couple's conversation, Talia said, "My mom's birthday is soon. I want you to get her a gift."

Talia then went on to describe the gift in detail, and where to buy it. What's remarkable is that she described not only the store, which had not even been in existence when she was alive, but the woman who had opened the store, where it was, and what it sold, giving the couple a detailed description of the item she wanted them to buy me. Right after they finished speaking with Rebecca, the husband got in the car and drove to that store, and on the table in the center of the room was the exact thing Talia had described. He bought it on the spot.

Yet another unbelievable event happened while Rebecca was shopping. She was looking at some necklaces, and as she passed one in particular she heard Talia's voice say, "Buy that for my mom, it's her birthday." Rebecca asked, "Talia, is this you?" "Yes, buy that for my mom." Rebecca bought the necklace, then called me and said she had something for me. I went to see her and had a reading, and it was then that she gave me the necklace Talia had picked out for me. It was made of crystals and stones; the meaning of one of the stones was "spirit manifestation." Another coincidence? Not in the least. It was Talia.

After hearing these messages and being blown away at the interconnectedness of them all, I had no doubt in my mind or heart or soul that Talia was sending them to me as signs that her consciousness was alive and with me still. As a reader who doesn't know Talia or me and has not lived our lives, you will never really feel the truth that I know so well. I'm telling you that before this time, I didn't believe in God, in the soul, in the spirit world. To convince me that Talia is still here, communicating with me, took some really big substantiations. Really big.

Chapter Eighteen

Talia Before Panama

Even before the plane crash that killed Talia, events occurred that would reveal unseen forces at work.

Talia had just turned thirteen a few weeks before leaving for Panama with her dad for their fateful weekend vacation, taking her friend Frankie with her. This wasn't the first time Talia had gone down to Panama with Michael—in fact, she had been there many times before. Michael went down to the islands at least twice a month, often taking Talia with him on his jaunts. Talia would surf, scuba dive, swim, explore, and commune with nature.

This particular trip was special to Talia because she was taking her friend with her. When I look back on it, what seemed like the beginning of a normal vacation was just a steppingstone on her soul's path, which she walked throughout her life. A life that, despite ending in the flesh, has not ended in spirit.

On December 19, 2007, when Talia's dad picked her up for the weekend, I kissed and hugged her goodbye, as usual. I told her to be safe and that I would see her in a few days. That was it. I didn't consciously know that the hug and kiss I gave Talia as she left were going to be the last I would give her while she was living, or that this moment would be the last time I would ever see her alive.

I say consciously because when I look at some of my actions and thoughts in the weeks prior to Talia leaving, and when I think about what has happened since the accident, it seems I somehow knew that Talia wasn't coming home—at least in my subconscious awareness. There's no way I could have known consciously and not held onto Talia and kept her from leaving that night.

One odd thing that happened was that just a week before Talia left for Panama, I told her I wanted her to organize her jewelry. At this point Talia had her earrings and other miscellaneous things scattered in different drawers. I wanted her real jewels to be kept in one safe place so they wouldn't get lost. Most of her jewelry had sentimental value more than anything else, but it was important to me that she keep track of it.

So one night I gathered all her jewelry, and together we went through it, figuring out what was what. We put all the important pieces in a little jewel box separate from her other things. That alone wasn't a big deal.

Then, a few days after Talia had left for Panama, I went to my safety deposit box and took out all my jewelry and other sentimental items and organized them, labeling everything for Talia—this came from her great-great grandmother, this was her grandfather's, and so on. If something happened to me, I didn't want Talia to be stuck with a bunch of things, mostly heirloom pieces, and not know the significance of each piece or who gave it to me and when. I cleaned it all up for her—or so I thought.

OK, maybe I was in an organizing frenzy or something. But looking at it now, there's no way I would have been able to go through Talia's jewelry after she died. It would have sent me over the edge, though at some point I would have had to. For some reason I was made to do it ahead of time. It seems very odd to me.

Then, while Talia was on her trip, I had a very strange "vision." I imagined Talia called me from Panama and told me that something had happened to her dad, and that she and Frankie were OK. I told her to stay exactly where she was; I was heading down to Panama right then to get her. Not to move—I would be there.

I figured this vision was just my imagination, and I actually forgot about it until soon after my return from Panama. But as I thought more about it, I realized it *had been* Talia, telling me she was OK, right after the accident. Her spirit letting me know she was OK. That made me very happy because when I first got back from Panama, I wondered why I hadn't "felt" the accident when it happened. There are so many stories of parents or spouses who say they had a strange feeling the moment an accident happened or an interesting visit from someone at the exact time the person died, and I wondered why I had not had that. I had even felt sad about not having had that feeling. But once I realized I actually *had* experienced it through my vision, I was a bit relieved. I can't explain why, I just was.

Of course, this vision was very close to what actually happened, just days later. Except that Talia didn't call me; someone else did.

When "the Call" came on December 23, one day before Talia was supposed to come home, I was propelled into a different realm, a place that I will never return from. Now, my entire belief system—my understanding of death and of the life I led with Talia and the life she's leading now—is different than I ever thought it would be.

How could her "death" change how I look at the life we had together? Her "death" forced me to analyze every single decision I had made in raising her, everything we had done together, and every single word I had ever said to Talia while she was growing up. I questioned every single move I had made and how it related to her. Had I made the right decision letting her show her horse so much? Had I done the right thing saying no to this and yes to that? It didn't stop. I questioned everything.

Looking back, I realized that how I raised Talia made her the person she was while here with me and prepared her perfectly for the next part of her soul's journey, her life after the accident. In fact, Talia herself sent me a message letting me know that how I had raised her is what made her the person she was on earth and the spirit she is now; it gave her the ability to be at the level she is now at, learning all that she's learning.

Here are the exact words she sent me through my friend G., who ended up having a great many communications with Talia. They are the words that helped me most:

Tell her my time there was divine. She did everything in a perfect way and was (is) an awesome mother. She got me here perfectly.

My mom got me here perfectly. That's why she has no regrets, as she shouldn't, ever. She will share in this reward, and it's far beyond tremendous. There are no words to describe it.

Those words are Talia's. When she said, "She has no regrets," she even used the words I had said just days before. A couple of days before Talia communicated this to G., I had told another person I had absolutely no regrets regarding my time with Talia. So when she said those words, it confirmed two things for me. One, that Talia is with me all the time, listening to me, and two, that I was in fact the best mother I could have been to her. All my questioning stopped. This is what gives me a sense of peace.

Talia Before Panama

Talia; Alaska summer 2006

CHAPTER NINETEEN

REMEMBERING

Raising Talia was my sole purpose in life. I loved being a mom more than anything else in the world, and I worked hard to raise her well.

Looking back at Talia's life here with me, I'm confident that I accomplished my goal. I know this because Talia was an amazing child and person, an independent-minded, analytical, gracious, joyful, generous, and thoughtful girl who was wise beyond her years. Yes, I'm her mother, and all mothers think their kids are the greatest, smartest, most perfect kids on earth. But I'm not the kind of person to give credit where it's not due—in fact, I'm pretty critical. So when I say that Talia was everything I said she was, it's true.

Here's a portion of something the head of Talia's upper school said about her at her memorial. I think it really exemplifies who Talia was from an outsider's perspective:

> The first time I met Talia, I was struck by her extraordinary independence, her contemplative focus, her philosophic composure, and her unflappable maturity. She was *two* at the time!

Every parenting book ever written, of course, refers to this time in the toddler's life as "the terrible twos," which makes my first memory of Talia all the more remarkable. Here was a child who, after being out of the womb and out in the world for just twenty-four months or so, comported herself with thoughtfulness, self-assurance, and grace— qualities that would become quintessentially Talia over the years.

Reading through Talia's school file and reminiscing with her lower-school teachers affirms that she was phenomenal from the get-go at Crane. Talia's first-grade teacher, for example, declared that "even if a comet landed in the soccer field and the class was going wild with commotion," she could rely on Talia to remain calm, stay on task, and do the right thing.

When Talia was in fifth grade, she exhibited such organizational prowess that she had her rough draft of a paper on Elizabeth Blackwell ready to turn in before Mr. C. even assigned an outline to help with the writing of the rough draft!

Talia continued to be a paragon of poise and a model of efficiency as an upper-schooler at Crane. Ask any seventh-grader to name a student with whom they liked to be paired for group work, and I'm certain that Talia's name will come up. In fact, Talia's classmates have been regaling me with Talia stories these past few weeks. Here's a common theme I sensed: When teachers assigned kids to work in groups, and kids found out they were partnered with Talia, they knew they had scored! One student said that with Talia as your lab partner in science, you simply got better results.

Another classmate noticed that you could usually get Talia to do all of the work, especially if you weren't very good at a particular subject, as was the case with this boy in art. A third student remarked that if something about the assignment wasn't perfect, Talia would redo the whole thing for the group, as she had done on a recent Spanish project.

Talia's capacity for work and her ability to get the job done wasn't limited to intellectual pursuits, however. She was just as masterful in social situations as she was in academic ones. Take, for example, her unofficial role as dance-floor captain. Several guys told me last week that when Talia would notice all the girls on one side at a party and all the boys on the other side, she'd pluck reluctant kids from the sidelines one by one, until absolutely everybody was dancing and having a blast.

When you're a teacher, you spend a lot of time wondering what your students will be like as adults. Sometimes it's difficult or even impossible to imagine what some kids will be like as grownups. This was never the case with Talia. She went about her business at Crane with such efficacy and aplomb that it was as though we had already had a glimpse of the adult Talia. Indeed, she figured out and accomplished more in thirteen years than many people do in a long lifetime.

Talia was true to herself. Everything she did was authentic and came from her heart, her soul, her true self. This is best seen through Talia's own writings. Here are some examples of her views about life, found in the autobiography she was assigned to write in school the year before the crash.

My Life Messages

Some of my life lessons have really helped me through a lot of situations. It took me a while to compile a list because there is a lot of big life messages that everyone should follow, like be kind and don't kill, but I tried to think of other life messages that people often forget about or put aside more often. The ones I chose could end up being a lot more important than you think in the long run. Here is what I chose:

1) Life isn't fair; don't think it is.
2) Be an optimist; believe the impossible.
3) Never give up; fight till the end.
4) Do what you believe is right; even if it means not going with the flow.
5) Believe none of what you hear and half of what you see.
6) Listen to your instincts; follow your gut.

Just One Day

I have thought long and hard about whom I would want to switch places with. I even wrote a paper on one person who I would switch places with. I read it to myself a couple of times. I decided that it was really horrible. I can't possibly imagine in my wildest dreams what it would be like to not be myself. I love my life so much I am lost when I try to think about what my life could have been.

Maybe for a day I could switch with the children in Rwanda so that at least for a day they could have a warm place to sleep, a meal, and clean water, so that they could live one more day. And maybe for one day I would really understand what it meant to suffer.

This chapter was the hardest for me but I am glad I did it. Maybe one day all little boys and little girls will have a warm bed to sleep in and food to eat every day. Not just for one day.

TALIA

Lively, friendly, hyper, smart
Sibling of Zippy, Gunther and Layla
Lover of ice cream
Who fear spiders
Who needs chocolate chip cookies
Who gives laughter
Who would like to see and travel the world
Resident of Sterling Silver Stables
Klein

Stop and Think: What is a Hero?

I think a hero is someone who is completely
selfless in all of their actions. Someone
who takes risks for others, and takes time
out of their own life for someone else's life.
I think that parents are heroes too,
because they raise us to be who we are
and put up with us when we're not so grateful.

(The "siblings" Talia referred to here were her dogs!)

Here's the letter Talia wrote to me when she was assigned to write a letter home, giving me a progress report on how she was doing in school.

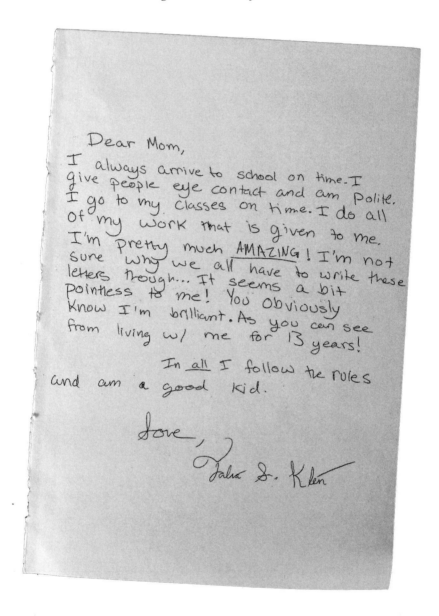

Dear Mom,

I always arrive to school on time. I give people eye contact and am polite. I go to my classes on time. I do all of my work that is given to me. I'm pretty much <u>AMAZING</u>! I'm not sure why we all have to write these letters though... It seems a bit pointless to me! You obviously know I'm brilliant. As you can see from living w/ me for 13 years!

In <u>all</u> I follow the rules and am a good kid.

love,

Talia S. Klen

Talia was truly a special person. Adults loved to converse with her. She was enthralled by conversations about the universe, whether there's a God, moral codes, quantum physics, music, literature, movies, food. She actually preferred to talk with adults than with most kids. But Talia was still a kid. She played sports, hung out with friends, loved volleyball, loved riding her horses and competing in horse shows.

Talia also was a great student, and she loved school so much that she was torn between missing school and going to horse shows. One time I wanted to take her to Magic Mountain on a school day, and she freaked out. No way was she willing to miss a day of school. It's not that I was a bad mom for wanting her to miss a day; it was just that Talia worked very hard and was always ahead in her assignments, so she was more than capable of missing a day of school for some good old fun. Even her teachers didn't mind that she "ditched" a day here and there for horse shows or whatever came up.

There was something unique about Talia. People called her an "old soul." She was truly that. She emanated wisdom.

Talia decided for herself that she didn't believe in God. That wasn't something I ever told her. Her father and I didn't believe in God, but I wasn't going to put my thoughts into Talia's head. She had to think for herself. It's interesting, though, that her belief system started to change as she neared thirteen.

Growing up, Talia would tell me that some of her dreams came true: sometimes she would dream that an event would occur, or that this or that would happen, and then it would actually happen, quite soon after her dream. She asked me if this was possible. Of course it's possible, I told her, because it's happening.

Well, those prophetic dreams of hers led her to start thinking about the possibility that there was more to us, more to the universe, than just our bodies. There was something else going on. Talia started to ask whether people could see into the future, and she said if that was possible, then maybe there were souls, or some sort of energy that enabled people to do this, since our regular bodies alone didn't have this ability.

Then Talia asked if I thought there were spirits all around us that we couldn't see but that animals could. This thought was spurred by Laura, an animal communicator I hired on instinct to "talk" to one of Talia's horses, Justinian, who sometimes acted up with her. When Laura "spoke" with Justinian and we heard what he had to say, both Talia and I were amazed. That conversation actually started Talia on an entirely new path and changed her understanding of the world.

When Talia realized that the animals were thinking, talking, and communicating with people and other animals, she concluded there must be a consciousness beyond the body. If that was the case, maybe there were spirits and other consciousnesses all around us, living in a world we couldn't see but that was truly there.

It was at this time that Talia asked about parallel universes—what were they, and did they exist. I told her I wasn't able to give her any real answers about whether they existed or even what they were, but there were scientists, quantum physicists, who were studying that very topic. Now that Talia was able to put a title to something she was so fascinated with, she decided, on the spot, that she wanted to become a quantum physicist instead of a patent litigator.

This revelation, as I called it, happened two weeks before Talia left on her final trip to Panama. It's amazing to me that right after Talia's mind was opened to the possibility that there's more to the world, life, and the universe than what we see, she left her body and moved on into the realm she was so curious about.

The timing of Talia's death may seem coincidental, but, looking at the psychic preparation she went through and her interest in topics well beyond her years—even beyond most adults' thought processes—it seems that she was preparing for her next adventure: her life in the afterlife. In fact, now that I have the benefit of hearing from Talia from her new life, I realize that is exactly what she said had happened.

It's extremely hard for me to think that Talia was only supposed to be here with me for a short time. But when I heard from Talia herself that her life here was in preparation for her life there, I realized that my life's purpose was indeed to raise Talia in a way that prepared her for where she is now. Her true purpose in the afterlife is to learn and to transmit the messages and lessons found in her communications to me and to the world. I have no doubt that I helped her accomplish that purpose. In Talia's own words:

> *My mom was very, very mindful of how she raised me. Do you see the fruit of it? She WILL share in the rewards of the fruit of my life, of my "being" who I am, because she was instrumental in it and a central part of my life. . . . It has nothing to do with my great honor of being her daughter or of my affection and LOVE for her as my mom. My love for her has no bounds and she knows this. I said before you had to be outside to see in; there are much deeper truths here than is readily apparent.*
>
> *The life I lived WAS for an example. I didn't know it then and if you would have told me I would have laughed. I wouldn't have thought that was necessarily true, but it was necessary and it was true. You may not always know whom you are influencing. I influenced people then without noticing it. You're always more than you think you are. But to know that is to trust it, that you can be used in a divine way whether you know it or not.*

I know in my heart that because Talia was educated in a way that enabled her mind to remain open to the possibilities of the universe, she was able to enter the next phase of her soul's journey at a very high level. This has allowed her to learn the lessons she has learned so far extremely quickly, and it has enabled her to move close to the source of all things. This high level of learning in the spirit world is what allows her to know what she now knows and, even more important, it allows her to be able to communicate that information to us here, in this earthly realm.

Talia; self portraits taken on her computer

Talia and I in Alaska summer 2006

Talia and Frankie, Fall 2007

Talia, at her 13th birthday party, wearing "THE" bracelet I gave her for Mother's Day, the one she wanted me to get off of her body.

CHAPTER TWENTY

TALIA'S WORDS

Talia's first messages to me, telling me she was OK, have expanded to include words of wisdom, love, and universal truths spoken and entrusted to the friend I call G. When G. asked Talia what she wanted him to do with these lessons of life, she said she wanted them to be published so everyone would be able to read them. So, following her wish, G. and I have put all of Talia's messages into another book called *The Universe Speaks: A Heavenly Dialogue.*

But the messages that follow have special meaning for me. Talia is communicating with G., and her words are exaclty as G. heard Talia speak them. Sometimes the meaning is open to different interpretations. But I'm not going to include the meanings G. and I glean from Talia's words; I'm leaving it to each person to find their own meaning. That is what Talia wanted. Each message has special meaning to each person and where they are in their life at that time.

I don't doubt, I don't question, and I'm not even a bit skeptical that they are indeed Talia's words, spoken by her to us, from where we call Heaven.

Talia, you had a perfect life.

It is even more perfect where I am now. My mom is being healed.

Where I am is more beautiful than where you are by a billion times. Where I am it is perfect perfection. There are horses here.

Tell my mom I love her.

She knows.

Just call her and tell her I love her. What is more important than that.

My mom showed me how to be free, to think your own thoughts and not what people tell you to think. If you're thinking someone else's thoughts, how can you be free? It's your birthright to be free. It's a yearning everyone has. So why would someone make a prison for others to live in?

People are enslaving each other on the earth. This needs to stop. Most of them aren't even aware of what they're doing to themselves and each other.

We used to walk and talk a lot. Ask her what we talked about. That will make her think. RE-MEM-BRANCE. Tying all the pieces together into one coherent whole. Piecing it together. Nothing is really apart except for the contrast of the separation.

I LOVE my friends and I'm sorry my going hurt them. It has purpose.

My ashes were my essence THERE.

Do you want me to carry them with me?

Talia's Words

Yes. My mom does.

Tell her hi . . . and I love her. This is her first Mother's Day without me.

My life went perfectly, perfectly.

Of all the misconceptions, death is the biggest myth of all.

The last enemy to be destroyed will be [our perception of] death. That's what we're attempting to get across here, that myth, that illusion of separation. There really is none. A lot of people know this. A lot of people think it's mere fabrication. The fabrication is the walls they've built with their mind. Matters not whether they believe they are creative beings or not, the fact is they ARE, therefore they ARE going to create, no matter WHAT they believe.

There is no age—a person's "essence," what they really are, is without time. Time OUT OF MIND. The age you speak of is an outward appearance or a chronological time line. It doesn't exist here. It is realized as a concept to be used here to put things in context to be understood there.

Death as you UNDERSTAND it is a myth, a concept. This misunderstanding is what hurts the most. That's why I told you as you looked at my ashes, "I'm not there," because I'm not, I'm "here." I'm as you said, the most alive person you know. That's why you've never heard me talk about my dying because I never did. That's an illusion and a myth, a very convincing one by the way.

It does hurt.

Yes, it does.

Thank you for telling J. I love him.

Do you know how many want this and from this side too, just to let their loved ones know they are all right. If there were envy here they would be envious. I'm telling you they are standing in awe of this.

You let my mom know from the beginning of this that I was OK, and that confirmed to her without a doubt that what she already knew was true, and I'm so thankful for that.

There's nothing else I could have done.

Yes, you could have ignored me.

Talia, you were so totally adamant about it I couldn't ignore you.

Yes, you could have. We're in a position to see the things people ignore and you would find it hard to believe. Talk about exasperation. If you knew how many times we shake our heads. "Why can't they see!" I've heard this many times. Many are so locked into their own little world that they cannot see what's really there. So I want you to know that I appreciate what you've done for me and are still doing.

I wouldn't have it any other way. This is a tremendous honor for me.

That's one reason my dad thinks so highly of you. He says he wishes he could have known you there.

Well, I appreciate that. Tell him thanks and I wish him the same thing.

He says to tell my mom he never wished to do any harm and if he had it to do over things would be different.

She'll read this.

He knows that.

Talia's Words

My heart aches.

I have a new life now. My old life has passed away, because energy can never be destroyed and energy is what we ARE.

Death as they see it is not death at all but of the body; it's a wonderful new beginning. You KNOW who I am. You also know who I was and you see glimpses of what I'm becoming.

I feel Michael's presence.

He has deep regret and feels responsible. He wants to talk to you and get his side of the story out there. It's not part of the message but I told him I would.

I told him he is not responsible and that things happen for a reason. He says he knows that and that he understands the importance of the message, but he feels the hurt and pain and sense of loss to those on earth.

At first he felt he had robbed me of my life on earth by his pride, but he now knows I'm where I need to be to help others in the greatest way possible.

He's not too happy with the way his father is acting towards mom, and he wishes he could get through to him and things were different.

He says the hardest thing for him now is not being able to communicate with those he needs to.

He says to tell you again how much he appreciates what you're doing with me.

Other than those things he's doing fine, but those issues have been very difficult for him.

Be at peace, Michael.

Thank you.

I heard him.

Yes, you did. He's growing and he does know God's peace.

Why . . . ?

It's clearer for you if I speak.

Some won't believe it, but this hasn't been done before, not on this level, not in this depth. People have been communing with "spirits" ever since there were people in the physical realm, but it hasn't been recorded in this depth before. Mostly it's been "bits and pieces."

Now I want to tell you of a not-so-well-kept secret, other than people keep it a secret from themselves. And that's our communication. A large part of this message is how to. How to communicate [between the physical and spiritual worlds]. If people will look at this as "bilateral communications" it will be much easier to grasp. The gulf that separates, as it were, is an invention of the mind of man. "Bilateral" meaning the symmetrical other side. I said before that the physical has a spiritual counterpart and to know yourself and the importance of that, and that if you did know yourself, others wouldn't be such a mystery. Well, to know yourself is to also know your spiritual counterpart and to call it unto yourself; after all, it's YOURS.

Talia, tell me about your prophetic dreams.

I had them a lot. Things would come to pass and there was no denying or explaining it. It made no sense to me at first. Then, as my awareness of what was happening grew, I knew there must be a soul and a Supreme Being. How else could it be explained? It did get and keep my attention on seeking how and what was happening. I knew there was more, there had to be, there was just no denying it. Then I felt the spirit at times. I didn't know what it was then but it felt larger than life. And that's what you saw in my eyes, the spirit that was larger than life itself, a window into the marvels of the universe. You literally looked into my eyes and saw the universe.

When you think of me, think of the celebration of life, not sorrow over the illusion of death. Death has no place here, it just does not exist. It's a state of mind, so don't put your mind in that state.

Death is not the end; it's a wonderful new beginning.

How so?

Every aspect of our life, every minute detail is reviewed and learned from—every failure, every success, every relationship you had—and didn't but should have. Everyone you helped and everyone you didn't help. Every kind word and every harsh or hateful statement. Every single detail will be reviewed and learned from. The growth this creates, the wisdom this generates is stupendous. Every word you've used will be judged. Even a kind thought is rewarded, for thoughts are life. There is time enough here; there's so very little there.

Chapter Twenty-One
NOW

When I first started writing this book, I was coming from a totally different place from where I am now, as I sit and write this final chapter. I first started typing as a way to regain my memory after I got "the Call." As I was going through the entire search and rescue process in Panama, not knowing whether Talia was dead or alive, my body and mind were not fully connected. I was physically functioning, but my emotions were not allowed to surface while I dealt with the horrific situation and the task before me—to find my daughter's plane and get her out of there. Wherever "there" was.

Even when it was clear that Talia and her father had not survived the crash, it didn't register, not for quite awhile. So, when I finally was cognizant of the truth, that Talia was gone, I freaked out because I couldn't remember anything. Not a thing about her or our life together. I knew that in order to recover my memories of my daughter, I would first have to deal with what happened in Panama.

I sat down and started typing. I wrote a moment-by-moment sequence of events, from when I first got the call that Talia's plane was missing until I arrived back in the United States, carrying her ashes in my backpack.

During that first phase of what turned out to be a chronicle of my life and beliefs, the memories became more vivid, and the moments I had been blocking out started to show back up in my memory bank. It was extremely helpful for me to be able to piece together all the events in order to try to come to terms with the reality that Talia was gone.

Once I had all the facts down, I just kept writing. The situation that had caused a total shift in my belief system didn't disappear the moment I stepped back onto U.S. soil. In fact, the events that followed my return home turned out to have as much impact on me as the crash itself had.

I wrote about everything, from my arrival back home, alone, without my daughter, to Michael's family's horrible treatment of me, to the way Michael was raised and how that had made him the man he was. Then about how Talia's continued existence in my life and her communications and lessons from another dimension literally changed my beliefs, and my life, forever.

As I continued to write about different aspects of my life and Talia's, I gained an understanding of how everything that happens in life and after our body ceases to exist is truly interconnected. I realized that there is a reason for every situation. One lesson is meant to be learned at a particular moment, and each of life's lessons build on and confirm each other, explain each other. This realization ultimately led me to formulate an overall understanding of life and the afterlife.

It is very clear to me that there are no coincidences, no accidents. Everyone's destiny is charted out, and regardless of what you do during your life on Earth, your destiny will be fulfilled.

This is not to say that people have no control over their lives along the way. They do have choices, as Talia points out in some of her communications with G. But no matter what path you choose or what actions you take, your destiny is set in stone.

It is quite clear to me that Talia was meant to leave this world and move on to another dimension when she did, and if I had known this and tried to stop it, the end result would not have changed, only the method of transition. This can be said about everyone. Our final destiny is planned out for us; it is how we get there that we can control to some extent.

I see this universal force at work when I look at the interconnectedness of all the events, lessons learned, people met, and places traveled that were part of Talia's experience. Take my actions just weeks before the crash, when I was in an organizational frenzy. I intuitively knew something was going to happen; I just interpreted it to mean that I had to prepare everything for Talia for when I "died." In no way would I have thought that it was Talia who was leaving. The timing of Talia's becoming open to a new way of thinking was no coincidence, either. She went from not believing in God to questioning and wondering about death, souls, and parallel universes, all during the few months before the crash. The people Talia met during this time period are, interestingly enough, now connected to her spiritually in some way.

One woman comes to mind in the context of a meeting that was definitely not accidental. Just weeks before the crash, at a Christmas party in December 2007, I met a woman who has since become a good friend. We were talking about private schools, and she told me she had met Talia when she and her daughter visited Talia's school. I thought it was such a coincidence that my first response was, "No way, you didn't meet Talia," but she insisted that she had in fact met her.

It turns out that she and her daughter were walking around the campus looking for a restroom. Talia was walking nearby, and the woman asked her for directions. Not only did Talia show them where the restroom was, but she walked them to it and talked to the mom while she waited for her daughter. Then Talia walked them to their next destination at the school. When my friend told me about this, I was sure it was Talia, just from hearing about her kindness. This was confirmed when my friend saw a photo of Talia in the paper while the missing plane situation was in the news. Yes, the helpful student had indeed been Talia.

What is really interesting is that this friend had lost her husband on 9/11. He was one of the heroes who tried to overtake the terrorists on Flight 93, and who died doing so. Now, here was a woman whose husband was trying to help others and who died in a plane crash. Here was Talia, who was trying to help others and who died in a plane crash. Two beautiful souls on earth, helping each other's families, both ending up at a high level in the afterlife.

Talia's death forced me to become more open, like she was. Before the crash, I was convinced that most people were selfish, and, honestly, I didn't want much to do with anyone. I spent time with a very tiny circle of friends, and that was it. I didn't want anyone else around.

But the moment news that the plane was missing got out, my desire to stay distant from people changed, immediately. It wasn't that I decided to open up because I now needed help. It was that the amazing outpouring of love and support—shown throughout my nightmare ordeal by friends, acquaintances, and people I had never met before in my community and around the country—opened my eyes to the true generosity and helpfulness

214

of these people. I was truly shown the interconnectedness of all human beings, whether we are aware of it or not.

This universal force of interconnectedness is always present in Talia's communications. You've already read about some of her messages through Rebecca and through G., but what I didn't point out is that every single communication with one source is always confirmed by another. Rebecca once saw Talia with a little girl, for example, and G. also saw Talia with a little girl. The communications that Laura, the animal communicator, had with Gunther, my dog who passed away, also matched up to things Talia had told G. in her communications. Even the smallest signs that Talia sent to me or to G., or even to my mother via Rebecca, were always consistent with signs she sent to other sources.

A precious example was when Talia showed her teeth to Rebecca and told her that I had not wasted money on her braces, since now her teeth were straight and perfect. Some time after that, I had a phone meeting with a famous medium in New York, and he told me that Talia was showing him her teeth and pointing to how beautiful they were. It doesn't surprise me that Talia was so adamant about showing me her beautiful teeth; she had just begun to wear braces six months before the accident and was always talking about what she would look like when they came off.

Even the smallest signs have meaning. Rebecca told me in a meeting at one point that I had known G. for many ages—longer, she said, "than Winchester had been making guns and ammo." Though that is not long in the scheme of time, it had meaning because on that very day G. looked down while he was walking, and at his feet was a label from a box of Winchester ammunition. Now, that is beyond coincidence.

Talia has communicated literally hundreds of things that are absolute proof of her continued existence and confirmation that she is with me all the time. Right after Talia's memorial service, both Talia and Michael told Rebecca they were at the "celebration of life," which is what I called it, and that they were happy to see this person and that person there. Michael said he was surprised to see Josh there, but that it was nice.

Indeed, it was a surprise to me, too. Josh is my uncle-in-law. He is divorced from my Aunt Sherry, whom I had not seen in years. Talia had not seen Josh since she was two, and that was about the same time Michael had seen him last. He was the only Josh at her celebration.

Then Talia mentioned that she loved the red rose one of her friends had given me, and that both she and her dad loved the food at the party afterward. It was deli food, Talia and Michael's favorite. Talia also commented how much she liked the DVDs of her I showed at the ceremony and said she was glad I had played her favorite music.

I could go on and on and on with examples of proof that Talia is always with me and that even Michael is with me at times, and that their consciousness is alive in another dimension.

Through all the communications, signs, and non-coincidental occurrences that happened before and after the accident, it has been proven to me that everything in the universe is in fact interconnected, that everything happens for a reason, and that there is, no doubt, life after life.

If any part of the experiences I have put down here can help even one person deal with the loss of a loved one from this realm, then I have done what I set out to do.

Talia and Mom; our last photo together, taken December 2007
© **photography by Helene Glassman /www.imagerybyhelene.com**

Epilogue

Since Talia's body died, I have experienced the great shattering that opened me up instantaneously to a new belief system. I have become much quieter in my mind and have been working on hearing Talia myself. Since the plane crash I have wanted nothing more than to be able to communicate directly with my daughter, and now I can honestly say that I too can hear her.

As Talia stated many times in her communications with G., all people have the ability to communicate with the spirit world; they just need to believe, and to quiet themselves. She said that communication between the spirits and us is as normal and natural as any conversation that two people in our realm would have. I'm here to tell you she's right.

But until you actually experience it for yourself, there's always a bit of doubt. Honestly, even in the beginning there's doubt. You hear but you're not sure you're actually hearing; you think it's your imagination. There are many, many instances where G. expressed to Talia his doubt that it was she he was hearing. She constantly reassured him it was in fact she.

Then when I started to hear Talia, I too doubted. I asked her for confirmations over and over again—so much so that she probably was annoyed at me, though she never let on to that! I would say, "Talia, is this really you?" And within minutes, G. would tell me that Talia had asked him to tell me, "It was me."

How do I hear Talia? A bit like G. hears her. I hear her in my head. I hear her thoughts, in my voice but in her voice too. It's hard to explain, but I talk to Talia in my head, and I hear her responses in my head. The answers to my questions just flow, and when they flow I know it's she. When the answers cut off my questions, I know it's she. I don't even have to state my question in word form; I just think it, and before the thought is truly formulated, I hear her answer in my head. If I have to think about it, I know it's not Talia, but me. There's a big difference.

How was I able to start hearing Talia? First of all, I truly believed that I could and that I would. Belief is the ultimate requirement. If you doubt, you will not hear. Also, over the last year I have done a lot of work to get where I am. I went to spiritual healers who helped me open up my channels of communication and quiet my mind so I could hear Talia. I went into a quiet place in my mind, a sort of meditation, in order to be free of outside noise so that she could get through to me.

Going to these healers is not necessary; I just felt it would help me speed up the process of learning how to quiet myself and gain confidence in what I was hearing. At this point I have seen Talia and spoken to her, and in a couple of cases I have touched her.

Another thing I did this past year was to have my astrological chart read and compared to Talia's, to her dad's, and to G.'s. The results of that reading were stupendous.

First of all, Stephanie, the astrologer, pointed out to me where in *my* chart it showed that my daughter would die instantly, in the air, with her father. She had seen it when she read for me years ago, but because I hadn't asked about Talia, she hadn't told me. (I agree with her decision). Stephanie also pointed out where *Talia's* chart showed her dying in the air instantly with her dad. She then pointed out in Michael's chart where it showed he would die instantly in the air with his daughter.

When I saw the three charts together, it was undeniable. Then Stephanie showed me where G. had a direct communication link to Talia, *once she was in spirit,* which had opened up the moment Talia "died." Stephanie went on to tell me a great deal more about my purpose in life once Talia was in spirit, my relationship with Talia before and after the crash, my relationship with G., and Talia's relationship with G. *All of it* was already known by me, in my heart, but seeing it confirmed was mind-blowing.

Talia was and is the most important person in my life and always will be. She is still in my life; I know it for a fact, though her body is not with mine. I can't see her sitting next to me, or driving with me, or lying down with me. I can't take her to horse shows or to the movies, or hear her blasting her music from her room. I can't make her dinner, or see her sitting there, smiling at me. But I know she is with me, all of the time. She has told Rebecca, G., and me that she will always be with me, and she is. I feel her.

Sometimes I feel her more strongly than at other times, but I always know she is here with me. This is what I want people to understand, so that they too can feel at peace and know that their loved ones who have "died" are OK. Talia has said it herself a few times. People don't die; their spirit, their energy, is alive after the body dies, even more alive than when in the body. It's the separation between us (who are still here in our bodies) and the spirits we love (who are here also but without their bodies) that is hard for us to deal with.

Besides coming to realize that there is NO DEATH, I have also learned that no matter what our path, we all get to the same place. No matter what choices we make here on earth, while in this body, we really are on a path already set out for us. We meet whom we meet for a reason. We do what we do for a reason—especially if we know our soul, listen to our inner voice, and follow that voice in how we live and what we do. Our inner vision knows the truth, but it's not always easy for us to hear that inner voice and see that inner vision.

Being able to hear from Talia, either myself or though G., has changed my life. I can make it through the day, through the night, through the week, and somehow, I have made it nearly a year since the plane crash without really wanting to leave this world myself.

Being able to hear and speak to Talia, and knowing that she is with me and watching over me and helping me with my every endeavor is more than an inspiration to me, it gives me peace. She gives me peace.

AFTERWORD

Just months before my appeal was to be heard, the entire matter was dropped. I say *dropped*, not settled, because though the official documents filed with the court state that I did in fact settle with the defendants, Bob Klein and Michael's estate, the "settlement" was not really a settlement at all. This is what happened.

I received a call from my mother-in-law, Anne. She told me she wanted to give me a gift—money—so that I would be able to live a little easier. She said she'd been thinking about this for a very long time, and although it wasn't meant to be a settlement, she did want the lawsuit to go away. Anne was very clear that this money was from her and her husband, Bill—not from Michael's estate. In fact, Bob was clear that he wanted no part of this gift and would not contribute a penny.

When Anne told me that she wanted to give me money, I began to cry. Not because I was happy to get money—not at all. I cried because finally, after all this time, someone from Michael's family was acknowledging the loss of Talia. Not only that, it was Anne who was acknowledging her death. A mother. Michael's mom, who had experienced the loss of her child as well. At last, someone was thinking of me—Talia's mom. My loss and my relationship with Talia were no longer being ignored, degraded or forgotten. Finally.

Though I wanted to accept Anne's gift on the spot, I knew I had to run the offer by my attorneys. The entire transaction had to be handled correctly, because at this point I was liable for the trial costs to the other side. I could not unilaterally drop the appeal; I needed to have those costs waived.

After a lot of arguing about whether the gift was really a gift or a settlement in disguise, and negotiating to have the other side's attorneys' fees waived, we finally reached an agreement that enabled me to accept Anne's offer. The word *settlement* had to appear on court documents in order to legalize the withdrawal of the appeal and all associated causes of action.

I ended up with about two-thirds of Anne's gift. The remainder went to my attorneys, who had worked very hard for my benefit.

Finally, I was done. Talia's "death" was not forgotten, my relationship with Talia was acknowledged, and my role as a mother was respected. If it were not for Anne and her husband, Bill, this might not have occurred. Thank you, Anne and Bill.

About Kim Klein

Raised in Southern California, Kim Klein attended the University of California, Santa Barbara. After graduating with a B.A. in Political Science, attending law school and being admitted to the California State Bar, Kim worked with her then husband in real estate investments and their high-tech companies. After having her daughter, Talia, Kim became a stay-at-home mom, devoting all of her time to raising her only child.

Just after her thirteenth birthday, Talia was killed when the small private plane she was on crashed into the side of a volcano. The event devastated Kim's heart and shattered her entire belief system—and from the moment of Talia's death, Kim's motherly devotion shifted from raising Talia to learning to communicate with her in the afterlife.

Kim now spends her time writing about her experiences surrounding the death of Talia and the many communications between Talia from heaven and the spirit world to us here on earth in the physical. She is learning how to heal others from the grief of losing a loved one, as well as studying primitive living skills. She currently resides in Nevada, where she enjoys the peaceful desert scenery and continues on her path of healing, learning, and spiritual awakening.

Kim can be reached via her website, *www.kimberlyklein.com*

For more information about this book:
www.hummingbirdsdontflyintherain.com

To order Kim's other book, *The Universe Speaks,* go to
www.theuniversespeaks.com

RESOURCES

There are many gifted and powerful astrologers, mediums and psychics in the world. There are also a great number of not-so-gifted ones. Then there are the "fakes."

I have tried nearly every medium and psychic that's come across my path—from the world famous to those that advertise on the street. The people I've mentioned throughout this book are those that have proven to be extremely gifted, honest and reputable. Over time they have become my favorite sources of spiritual communications, guidance for my own awakening—and very special people in my life.

Though each client and reading is different, and everyone relates differently to different people, I am very comfortable recommending these people to my family, friends, and you, the reader. I want to help those of you that are searching for a way to communicate with your loved ones but don't know where to look for it. Providing these names and contact information is also way for me to give back to them for the great blessing they have been and continue to be in my life.

Astrologer

Stephanie Jourdan, Ph.D.
Astrologer, Author, Lecturer
Higher Self Communications, Inc.
Woodland Hills, CA
818-340-4099
www.HigherSelfCommunications.com
www.LifeIsAGiftShop.com
info@HigherSelfCommunications.com

Medium

RonaLaFae Thapa
ronalafae@msn.com

Pet Psychic

Laura Stinchfield
website *www.ThePetPsychic.com*
Laura@thepetpsychic.com

Hummingbird Artwork

Hummingbird art used on the cover was painted by Yin Ping Zheng, traditional Chinese painter and calligrapher. *www.yinpingzheng.com* 661-733-8333

Editor

This book was edited by Jennifer Read Hawthorne:
www.jenniferhawthorne.com
jennifer@jenniferhawthorne.com

Memorial and Celebration Jewelry

In order to keep a part of Talia with me physically, I had a few custom jewelry pieces made to hold her ashes. Everyone who saw these pieces loved them so I decided to offer them to the world.
www.memorialandcelebrationjewelry.com

I want to thank Randy Peyser of Author Onestop for all of her help and support.
www.authoronestop.com

You can read more of Talia's conversation
from Heaven in Kim's other book,
The Universe Speaks: A Heavenly Dialogue.

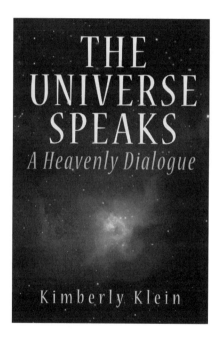

You can buy *The Universe Speaks* on the authors
website, *www.kimberlyklein.com,* at *Amazon.com,*
as well as from other retailers and online bookstores.